Move Beyond 4

STUDENT'S BOOK

macmillan education

Robert Campbell
Rob Metcalf
Rebecca Robb Benne

6 UNIT MIND AND BODY

IN THE PICTURE Create an avatar

>>> Talk about the human body

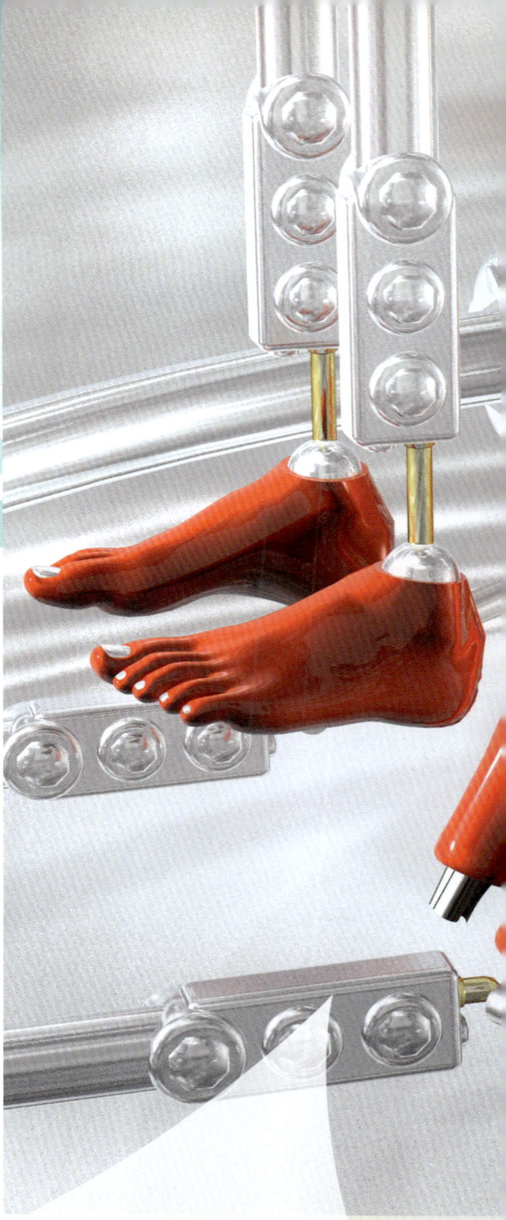

WORK WITH WORDS

1 RECALL In pairs, write the names of the body parts (A–L) in the pictures. You have one minute.

2 ▶01 Listen to the clues and match the words to the body parts (M–X) in the pictures.

...... ankle *M* brain ...... chest ...... finger ...... heart
...... knee ...... neck ...... shoulder ...... stomach
...... throat ...... thumb ...... toe

3 ▶02 Listen and check your answers. Then listen and repeat.

4 Write the body parts in Exercise 2 in order, from the highest to the lowest when you're standing up.
brain, ...

5 THE MOVING PICTURE ▶ Watch the video. Write the order in which the machine adds the avatar's body parts. What does the avatar do when it's complete?

6 Take the quiz. Then compare your answers with a partner.

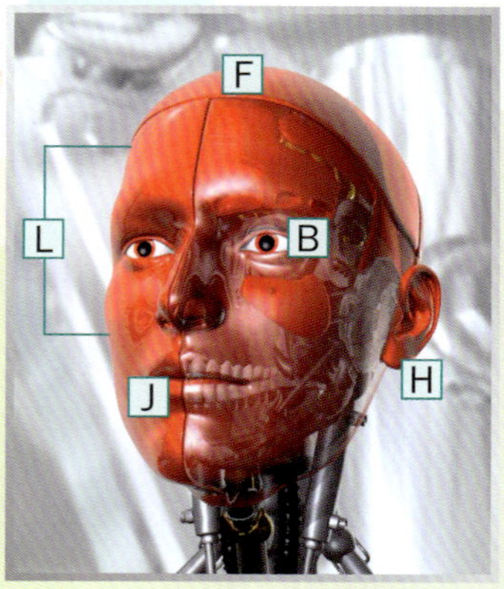

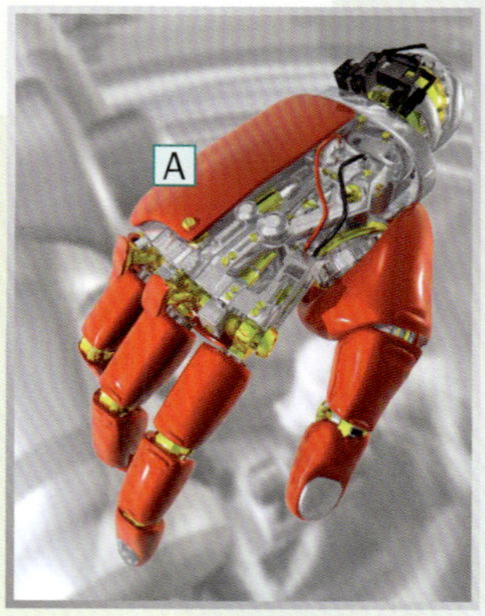

The Body Parts Quiz

How much do you know about the **human body**? Answer the questions.

1 It's the most complex object in the universe. What's it called?
2 It makes sure air and food goes to the correct place. What is it?
3 Two parts of our body get bigger and bigger, but we don't cut them. What are they?
4 Three bones connect here, including our biggest bone. What is it?
5 This part of our body can destroy metal. Which part?

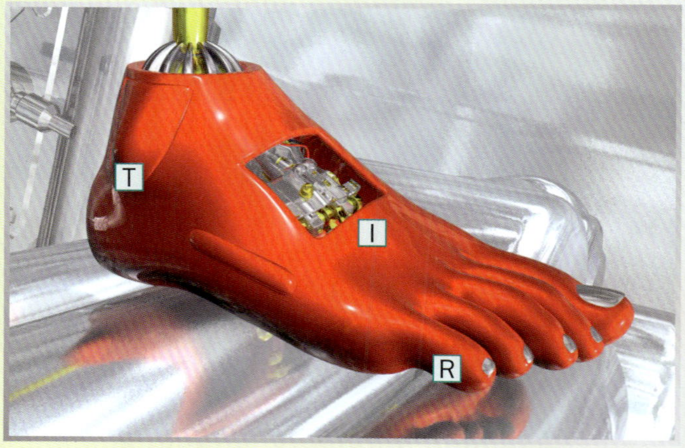

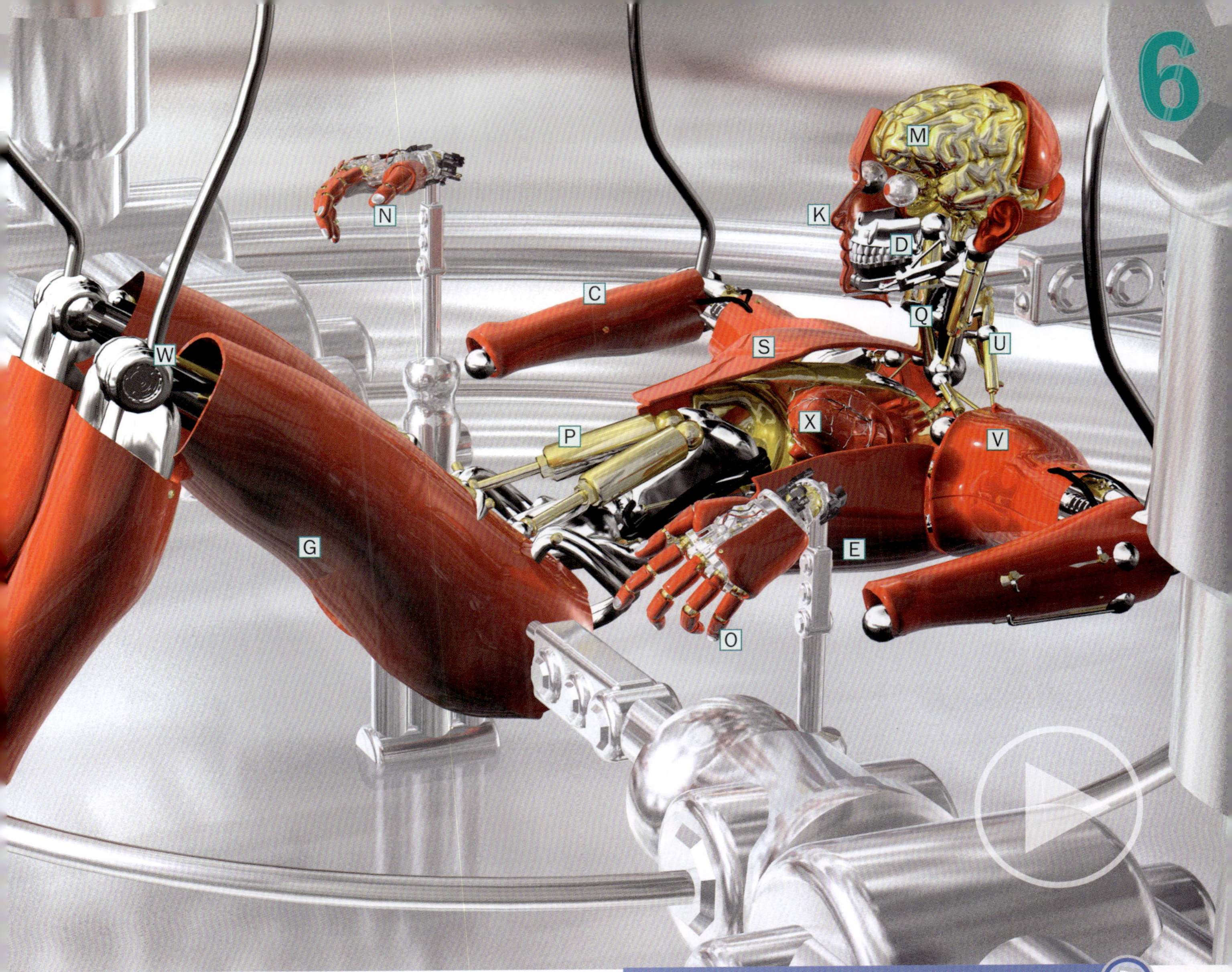

SPEAK

7 Draw an avatar, but don't let other students see it. Use the avatars below for ideas.

PHRASE BYTES

It has (a) big / small / long / short / round / square …

It has … next to / above / under / around its …

It looks like a …

Futuristic

Manga

Monster

Robot

8 Work in pairs. Describe your avatar to your partner. Can he or she draw it?

MOVE BEYOND

Do the Words & Beyond exercise on page 65.

Workbook, page 76

READING Train your brain

Read quickly

SPEAK AND READ

1 **Work in pairs. Talk about the activities below. Do you like doing them? Why or why not?**

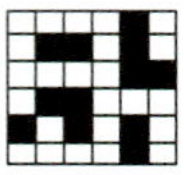
crosswords

Sudoku

chess

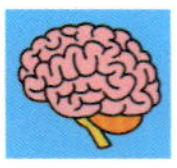
brain training games

PHRASE BYTES

I love / hate doing / playing …

It's / They're really relaxing / boring / difficult.

HOW TO

read quickly

- ☐ Read groups of words, not individual words.
- ☐ Don't stop if you don't understand a word or sentence.

2 **a** **Read the tips in the HOW TO box.**

b 03 **Quickly read the website homepage, but don't do the puzzles. Use a timer to see how fast you can read it.**

THE BRAIN PUZZLER

Logic puzzles | Word puzzles | Number puzzles | Quizzes | Games

Welcome to The Brain Puzzler, the best site on the internet for free brain puzzles! We have over 10,000 puzzles to train your brain and keep it working quickly.

Why should we do brain puzzles?

We all know the importance of eating a balanced diet. If we eat well, our whole body works better and we feel better. We all know how important it is to exercise regularly too. To have a healthy heart, we should exercise for 30 minutes at least three times a week. But did you know that our brain needs exercise too? We get a lot of our intelligence from our parents, but between 20 and 50 percent of our intelligence comes from how we use our brains. So if we regularly use our brains to do puzzles, we actually become more intelligent! Puzzles are a great way to get smart and have fun at the same time!

Try our top five! Click here to see the answers.

Not convinced? Try our all-time top five brain puzzles. Then click on the tabs above to find more puzzles.

1. If you are in a race and you pass the person in second place, what place are you in?
2. If 6 is equal to 11, and 8 is equal to 15, what is 11 equal to?
3. If you add two letters to this five-letter word it becomes shorter. What word is it?
4. In English, four days start with the letter "t." What days are they?
5. If 5 – 2 = 3, how can FIVE minus TWO be FOUR?

3 **Which tips in the HOW TO box did you use for help with Exercise 2b? Check (✓) them.**

4 **Can you remember the answers to these questions? Read the website again to check.**

1. How much does it cost to use the website?
2. How many puzzles are there on the website?
3. Why is it good to eat a balanced diet?
4. To have a healthy heart, how often do we need to exercise?
5. What happens if we do puzzles?
6. What other reason does the website give for doing puzzles?

5 **Do the puzzles. Compare your answers with a partner, then check them on page 141.**

REACT

6 **Work in pairs. What do you think? Tell your partner.**

1. Which puzzles were easy? Which were difficult? Why?
2. Do you think doing puzzles can make you more intelligent? Why or why not?

MOVE BEYOND

Make a list of other activities that are good for your brain. Which ones do you do?

Workbook, page 77

GRAMMAR Zero conditional, *should*

Talk about results and the best thing to do

READ Grammar in context

1 **Answer the quiz questions.**

Logic puzzles | Word puzzles | Number puzzles | Quizzes | Games

General Knowledge Quiz 1: Health

1. If you break your arm, it normally takes about … to get better.
   A 6–8 weeks B 6–8 months
2. If you don't want a cold, what should you do?
   A eat oranges B wash your hands often

STUDY

2 **Complete the example. Use Exercise 1 to help you.**

Zero conditional

Use the zero conditional to describe situations that are always true.

Use the simple present for the situation and the result.

If you ________ your arm, it ________ six weeks to get better.

See GRAMMAR DATABASE, page 60.

3 **Complete the examples. Use Exercise 1 to help you.**

Should

Use *should* to say that something is or isn't a good idea.

Affirmative and negative

should / *shouldn't* + verb

If you want to exercise your brain, you ________ do puzzles.

If he doesn't feel well, he ________ go to school.

Questions

should / *shouldn't* + subject + verb

What ________ you do?

See GRAMMAR DATABASE, page 60.

PRACTICE

4 **Complete the quiz questions with the correct form of the verbs. Then choose the correct answer.**

Logic puzzles | Word puzzles | Number puzzles | Quizzes | Games

General Knowledge Quiz 2: Science

1. Most things get … if you (1) *heat* (heat) them.
   A bigger B smaller
2. If you heat water at the top of Mount Everest, it (2) ________ (boil) at …
   A 100°C B 71°C
3. You (3) ________ (not need) to wear sunscreen if it (4) ________ (be) cloudy.
   A True B False
4. If you (5) ________ (leave) a refrigerator door open, (6) ________ (it / make) the room colder?
   A Yes B No

Workbook, pages 78–79

5 **a** **Choose the correct options. Then compare your answers with a partner.**

Logic puzzles | Word puzzles | Number puzzles | Quizzes | Games

General Knowledge Quiz 3: Dangerous situations

1. If you're in a storm, you should / (shouldn't) stand under a tree.

2. You should / shouldn't use the elevator if there's a fire in a building.

3. If you're on vacation in the USA and you need the police, you should / shouldn't call 911.

4. You should / shouldn't go swimming if you see a red flag at the beach.

5. If you burn your hand on something very hot, you should / shouldn't put ice on it.

b **Check your answers with your teacher. Write and ask questions.**

If you're in a storm, should you stand under a tree?

WRITE AND SPEAK

6 **a** **Work in pairs. Prepare an extra question for Quiz 1, Quiz 2, and Quiz 3.**

b **Exchange your questions with another pair and answer their questions.**

LISTENING AND VOCABULARY Stretch!

»» Understand spoken instructions

WORK WITH WORDS

1 Work in pairs. Answer the questions.

1 How often do you do exercise?
2 What exercise do you do? Where do you do it?

2 Match the exercise verbs in the box to the pictures.

___ hold	___ look down	___ look up	___ point
___ pull	___ sit down	___ stand up	___ stretch
___ touch	___ turn		

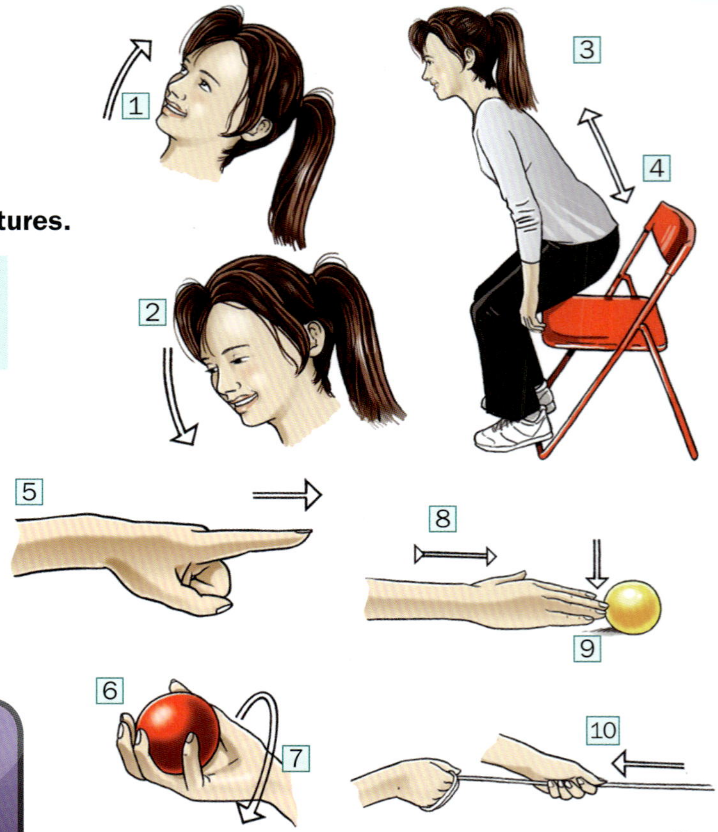

3 ▶04 Listen and check your answers. Then listen and repeat.

LISTEN

4 a Read the tips in the HOW TO box.

b ▶05 Listen to the podcast and do the exercises.

HOW TO
understand spoken instructions

- ☐ Listen for imperatives (*listen, don't talk*). They give instructions.
- ☐ Listen for sequencers (*first, next, then, now*). They tell you when a new instruction starts.
- ☐ Listen for adverbs (*slowly, carefully*). They tell you how to do something.

5 Which tips in the HOW TO box did you use for help with Exercise 4b? Check (✓) them.

6 ▶05 Listen again and fill in the missing information.

Exercise at your desk

The benefits:	You'll feel better and (1) ___*study*___ better.
Be careful:	It's important to do the exercises (2) ______ .
Exercise 1:	You're (3) ______ when you start this exercise.
Exercise 2:	This exercise relaxes your (4) ______ .
Exercise 4:	This exercise stretches your (5) ______ .

PHRASE BYTES

I feel OK, but my ... hurts.
I feel really good.
I don't think it's a good idea. We come here to study.
We don't have much space, but ...

7 Work in pairs. Invent a short exercise routine with a maximum of three different exercises. Use the verbs in Exercise 2 and the parts of the body on page 64.

REACT

8 Work in pairs. What do you think? Tell your partner.

1 Do you feel better after doing the exercises? Why or why not?
2 Do you think it's a good idea to exercise in class? Why or why not?

MOVE BEYOND

Do the Words & Beyond exercise on page 65.

»» Workbook, pages 80–81

GRAMMAR First conditional

Talk about possible situations in the future

READ Grammar in context

1 Read the conversation. What do Rosa and Aiden decide to do?

Rosa: Look at this. There's a fun run downtown next month. It says that if you finish the run, they'll give $20 to charity.
Aiden: I'm really out of shape. What will happen if I don't finish?
Rosa: It's only 5 km. If it's too far, just walk.
Aiden: OK. I'll do it if you do.
Rosa: Great. Who knows, we might win if we train!

STUDY

2 Complete the explanations with the correct tense.

First conditional

Use the first conditional to talk about possible situations and their future results.

Simple present or future tense
Use the ____________ tense after *if* to indicate the possible situation.
Use the ____________ tense to indicate the result.
If you finish the race, they will give $20 to charity.

You can use *may* or *might* (50 percent sure) and *will probably* (75 percent sure) in the result.
We might win if we train!
If we train, we will probably do well.

See GRAMMAR DATABASE, page 60.

PRACTICE

3 Choose the correct options.

1 If you *don't* / *won't* wear running shoes, you'll hurt your feet.
2 The charity will make money if your friends *do* / *will do* the run.
3 You *hurt* / *might hurt* yourself if you *don't* / *won't* stretch before the race.
4 If *it's* / *it'll be* a hot day, *you* / *you'll* need to drink a lot of water.

Workbook, page 82

4 a 06 PRONOUNCE **Listen to the sentences. Underlined the stressed words.**

If you finish the run, they'll give money to charity.
If you don't train, your legs will hurt the next day.

b 07 **Listen and repeat the sentences. Pay attention to the stress on the nouns, verbs, and adjectives.**

5 a Complete the opinions about the future with the correct form of the verbs.

1 "If you ____eat____ a balanced diet, you ____________ (**not live**) longer."
2 "You ____________ (**do**) better at school if you ____________ (**exercise**) regularly."
3 "Your brain ____________ (**work**) faster if you ____________ (**do**) lots of puzzles."
4 "If you ____________ (**not go**) to college, you ____________ (**not get**) a good job."

b Do you think the opinions are true? If not, change them. Use *will probably*, *might*, or *probably won't*.

If you eat a balanced diet, you might live longer.

6 Put the words in order to make questions.

1 this weekend / will / rains / you / What / if / do / it / ?
What will you do if it rains this weekend?
2 which website / go online / If / tonight, / you / visit first / you / will / ?
____
3 will / What / your English teacher / don't / your homework / do / you / do / if / ?
____
4 you / If / to the movie theater this weekend, / you / will / see / go / what movie / ?
____
5 if / all your tests / your mom or dad / What / pass / will / say / you / ?
____

SPEAK

7 Work in pairs. Answer the questions in Exercise 6.

PHRASE BYTES

I'll / I'll probably / I might ...
I'm not sure, but he / she / they won't ...
I really don't know.

LANGUAGE & BEYOND

>>> Communicate your message when you give a speech

COMMUNICATE & COOPERATE

READ AND LISTEN

Uh, hi. Should I start now? OK. Um. Where should I start ... uh ... Yes, well, you all know my hobby. Well, most of you.

1 Look at the photo of a student giving a speech and read the beginning of the speech. Do you think the speech went well? Why or why not?

2 08 Listen to Ruben's speech. What's it about?

3 Work in pairs. Answer the questions about the speech.

1 In general, do you think it was a good speech? Why or why not?
2 What could Ruben do to make his speech better? Think of two or three suggestions.

DO

4 Work in pairs. Look at the tips for giving a speech. Give each tip a point 1–5, where 5 = very important and 1 = not important.

____ Make eye contact with the audience.
____ Don't read the speech. Use notes, or cards with a few words on them.
____ Introduce the speech. Say what you're going to talk about.
____ Speak slowly and clearly.
____ Introduce all the sections in the speech.
____ Practice your speech. Give it to friends or family members.

PHRASE BYTES

I don't think it's important to ...

I think it's more important to ... than to ...

Do you think you should ... ?

I think it depends on the speech / audience / topic. If ...

REFLECT

5 Discuss the questions with your class. Do you agree with the REFLECTION POINT?

1 Which tips did you give 5 points to? Why are those tips important?
2 How do you think the other students felt during Ruben's speech? Why?
3 When was the last time you gave a speech in class? Did it go well? Why or why not?

REFLECTION POINT

To communicate your message well during a speech, it's important to prepare well, to speak clearly, and to look at your audience.

EXTEND

6 Prepare a one-minute speech about one of your hobbies or interests. Use the tips in Exercise 4 to help you.

7 Work in groups. Practice your speeches. Give other students suggestions for making their speech better.

Workbook, page 85

SPEAKING At the doctor's office

Ask for and understand advice at the doctor's office

SPEAK

1 Match the expressions to the photos.

___ a temperature ___ a sore throat ___ a headache
___ a cough ___ a runny nose ___ a stomachache

1

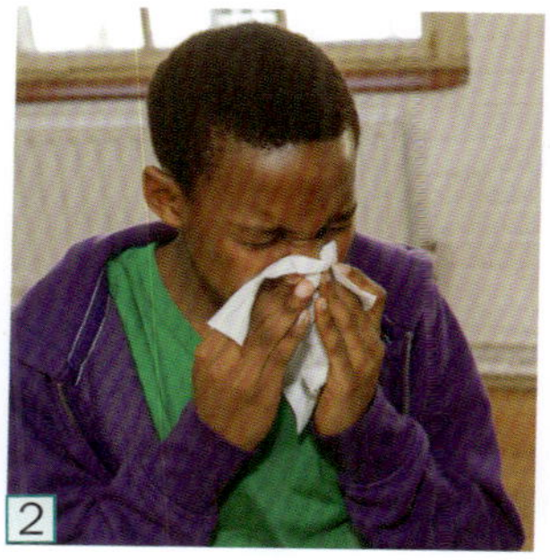
2

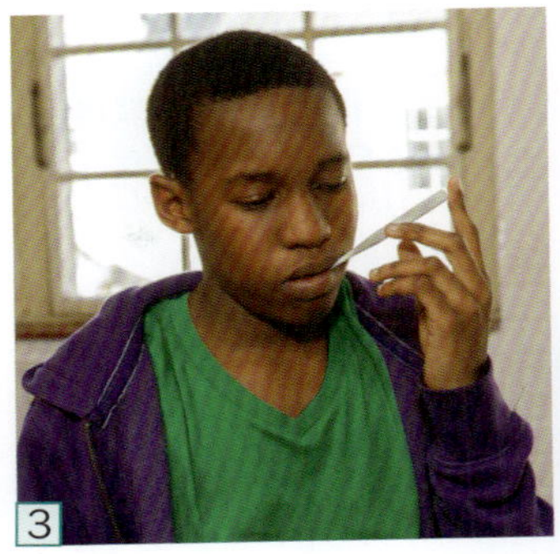
3

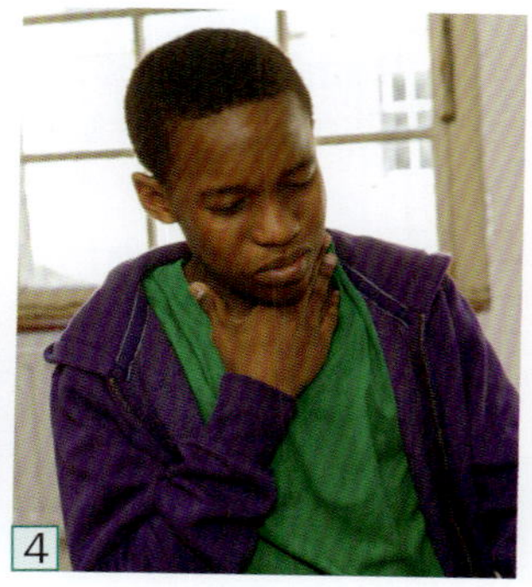
4

5

6

2 09 Listen and check your answers. Then listen and repeat.

3 Work in pairs. Answer the questions.

1 When was the last time you were sick?
2 Did you visit a doctor or a nurse? What did he or she say?

LISTEN

4 10 Kevin visits a doctor. Listen to the first part of the conversation. What are his symptoms?

5 11 Listen to the rest of the conversation. What does Kevin have? What does he need to do?

Doctor: I'm afraid you have the flu.
Kevin: The flu? So what should I do?
Doctor: Well, you shouldn't go to school. You should rest a lot.
Kevin: Should I take some medicine?
Doctor: I'm not sure that will help, but maybe you could take a pain reliever for your headache.
Kevin: I have a basketball game on Friday.
Doctor: I think you should probably stay at home.
Kevin: But I'm the captain!
Doctor: You won't be better on Friday, so maybe it'll be best for your team if you don't play.

6 a Read the tips in the HOW TO box.

b Underline examples of being sensitive in the conversation.

7 12 Listen and repeat the sentences from the conversation.

ACT

8 Work in pairs. Prepare a conversation at the doctor's office. Include expressions from Exercise 1 and ways of expressing advice in a sensitive way.

9 Practice and memorize your conversation. Then present it to other students.

HOW TO

be sensitive

- Use *I'm afraid* for bad news.
- Use *perhaps*, *maybe*, and *I think … probably* for difficult advice.

PHRASEBOOK 13

Say what's wrong

I have a cough / temperature / runny nose.
I have a headache / a stomachache / backache.
My head / stomach / back hurts.
I have a sore throat.

Ask for and give advice

Should I go / see … ?
What should I do / take?
Perhaps / Maybe you should …
Shouldn't you go / stay … ?
I think you should probably stay / take …

Workbook, page 75

WRITING What's your advice?

Give examples

SPEAK AND READ

1 **Read the problem and the replies on a forum. Which reply do you think gives the best advice? Why? Compare your answer with a partner.**

YOU.ME.US
Real problems. Good advice.

Forum | Login/Register

I recently moved to a new town. At first I missed a lot of things like my friends and my old room. I have a lot of new friends now, but school isn't going well. One girl in my class does really terrible things like telling lies about me. And she's mean during class too. For example, if I talk in class, she laughs. What should I do?
Paula
View comments • Like • Reply — Added 3 days ago

I think you should speak to your teacher. The school can do a lot of things, such as talking to her, or contacting her parents.
James
Like • Reply — Added 1 day ago

Perhaps you should talk to her. If you talk to her when she's not with her friends, maybe she'll tell you why she's being so mean.
Lidia
Like • Reply — Added 4 hours ago

2 a **Read the tips in the HOW TO box.**

HOW TO
give examples

- Use *like* and *such as* before a noun (*friends*) or *-ing* form (*telling lies*).
- Use *For example,* at the start of a sentence.

b **Underline examples in the forum messages.**

PRACTICE

3 **Write ONE word in each blank to complete another message on the forum.**

My problem is schoolwork. I just can't do it all. For (1) ____________, I have three tests next week, but I also have a lot of homework for hard subjects (2) ____________ math and physics. I have other things to do too, such (3) ____________ preparing to give a speech in class. I don't stop studying until 10 at night and then I can't sleep. What should I do?
Stefan

4 **Work in pairs. Decide on the best advice for Stefan.**

DISCUSS

5 **Discuss a situation that you want to change. Use one of these problems or think of a problem that's important to you.**

My parents don't understand me.
I feel really tired all day.
I can't stop worrying about things.

WRITE

6 **Write about a problem and ask for advice.**

1. Explain the problem in six sentences. Describe where you are, who you're with, and what you're doing. Write about ways you try to solve the problem.
2. Use the zero and first conditionals to talk about the results of different actions. Give one or two examples of the problem situation. *If I ask a question, everyone laughs.*
3. Give examples of the problem with *like*, *such as*, and *for example*. See the HOW TO box.

SHARE

7 **Exchange your problems with other classmates. Read other problems and reply to them with your advice. What's the best advice for your problem?**

Workbook, pages 84–85

VOCABULARY Parts of the body

1 Complete the parts of the body.

The Whole Body Workout!

The Whole Body Workout will benefit every part of your body, from your (1) ne _ _ , (2) th _ _ _ _ , (3) sh _ _ _ _ _ _ s, (4) ch _ _ _ , (5) he _ _ _ , and (6) st _ _ _ _ _ in the top half of your body, to the (7) f _ _ _ _ _ s and (8) th _ _ _ s on your hands and the (9) t _ _ s on your feet. Strong, flexible (10) k _ _ _ s and (11) an _ _ _ s will help you walk faster, and the exercises will help your (12) b _ _ _ _ think faster too.

___ /12

Exercise verbs

2 Complete the instructions with the verbs in the box.

hold look look point pull
sit stand stretch touch turn

"OK, you're sitting on the sofa watching TV. The commercials come on. Put on your DVD and move your body! First, (1) ________ up. Now you're on your feet, (2) ________ up. Can you see the ceiling? With your arms above your head, (3) ________ your fingers at the ceiling. Next, slowly (4) ________ your chest to the right. Then to the left. Now (5) ________ down. Can you see your toes? You're going to (6) ________ your toes next. Slowly move your chest forward. This will (7) ________ your back and the muscles in the backs of your legs. Are you there? If you can, (8) ________ your toes between your thumb and your fingers. Now (9) ________ your head down toward your toes. That's it! You can (10) ________ down again now and take a break!"

___ /10

GRAMMAR Zero conditional, *should*

3 Complete the advice with the zero conditional and *should* form of the verbs.

Work out – but take it easy!

We all know that we (1) ________ (exercise) regularly. If you (2) ________ (exercise) three or four times a week, your body (3) ________ (have) more energy. But you (4) ________ (not start) your workout without warming up first. If you (5) ________ (do) some stretching and light exercises first, it (6) ________ (prepare) your body for action. And listen to your body when you're exercising. It (7) ________ (be) time to stop if an exercise (8) ________ (not feel) comfortable.

___ /16

First conditional

4 Choose the correct options.

Sign up now!

(1) *You / You'll* get 50 more fantastic exercises if (2) *you / you'll* buy The Whole Body Workout 2. And if (3) *you / you'll* sign up for our internet service, (4) *you / you'll* have your own personal trainer. For just $5 a month, you'll be able to ask for all the help you need. And if (5) *you aren't / you won't be* completely happy after 30 days, (6) *we / we'll* return your money.

___ /12

Your score: ___ /50

SKILLS CHECK

✓✓✓ Yes, I can. No problem!
✓✓ Yes, I can. But I need a little help.
✓ Yes, I can. But I need a lot of help.

I can read quickly. ________
I can understand spoken instructions. ________
I can communicate my message when I give a speech. ________
I can ask for and understand advice at the doctor's office. ________
I can give examples when I write. ________

Workbook, pages 86–87

READ

1 **Read the text and choose the correct word (A, B, C, or D) for each blank.**

No need to run for fitness!

There was good news this week for "couch potatoes" – people like me who sit (1) ____________ soon after they get up, and spend all day sitting. I know I (2) ____________ probably go running. After all, exercise is good for the heart. It sends more oxygen to the (3) ____________ and that helps us think. The problem is, I'm really bad (4) ____________ sports.

A new study shows that walking (5) ____________ be better for your heart than running. Walking isn't so hard on the (6) ____________, so walkers get fewer knee problems. Plus, walking can help you stay in good (7) ____________.

However, you need to walk quickly (8) ____________ you want the full health benefits. You should (9) ____________ your legs and back first to prepare your body for action. Try bending down slowly and (10) ____________ your toes a few times before you start.

	A	B	C	D
1	**A** up	**B** down	**C** with	**D** as
2	**A** am	**B** can	**C** won't	**D** should
3	**A** brain	**B** neck	**C** throat	**D** chest
4	**A** in	**B** on	**C** for	**D** at
5	**A** it	**B** could	**C** probably	**D** to
6	**A** stomach	**B** shoulder	**C** body	**D** thumbs
7	**A** shape	**B** balance	**C** rhythm	**D** body
8	**A** so	**B** or	**C** if	**D** while
9	**A** stand	**B** hold	**C** stretch	**D** point
10	**A** looking	**B** touching	**C** turning	**D** stretching

Reading: ________ /10

TEST-TAKING TIPS

complete a multiple-choice text with blanks

- Quickly read the text. What's it about? What's its goal?
- Read it again. Think what the word for each blank might be.
- Look at the choices. Is your word there?
- If not, look at the other choices. Which word fits best?

LISTEN

2 ▶14 **You'll hear two students talking about brain training. Check (✓) the correct box for each question.**

1 Bart is trying to …
- A decide if brain training is for real. ☐
- B figure out an app on his phone. ☐
- C do a crossword puzzle. ☐

2 Candace likes to …
- A do Sudoku and crossword puzzles. ☐
- B play Chess. ☐
- C exercise and play basketball. ☐

3 Because exercise is important for your body, …
- A it doesn't seem important for your brain. ☐
- B it can give you a headache. ☐
- C it makes sense that it is important for your brain. ☐

4 Candace's mom thinks brain games …
- A help her with her memory. ☐
- B help her stay alert and focused. ☐
- C help her make better decisions. ☐

5 Candace and Bart decide to …
- A go out and play basketball. ☐
- B stay in and do a puzzle. ☐
- C find another brain game to play. ☐

Listening: ______ /10

TEST-TAKING TIPS

answer multiple-choice questions

- Read the instructions. What are you going to hear?
- Read the questions and choices. Underline important words.
- Listen. Decide which choices aren't possible.
- Listen again. Choose the best of the possible options.

WRITE

3 Complete the second sentence so that it means the same as the first. Use no more than three words.

1 I could help you study if you'd like.
Would you ______________ help you study?
2 Her plan is to give a speech on exercise next week.
She's ______________ on exercise next week.
3 It's a good idea to eat a lot of fruit.
You ______________ eat a lot of fruit.
4 If you want to win the race, you'll need to train a lot.
You'll only win the race if ______________ a lot.

______ /4

4 Some of your friends want to get together over the weekend and hang out. Write them a message (35–45 words).

- Say what you think the group *should* do on Friday and Saturday.
- Be sure to include some *shouldn't* phrases.
- Mention some conditional elements that might cause a change in plans.

______ /6

Writing: ______ /10

TEST-TAKING TIPS

write a message

- Read the task carefully. Who are you writing to?
- Plan your message before you write.
- Include phrases to start and end your message.
- Use *because* before a reason and *so* before a result.

Progress check score ______ /30

UNIT 7

TIME FOR WORK

IN THE PICTURE At work

>>> Talk about jobs and workplaces

WORK WITH WORDS

1 RECALL **Work in pairs. Write the workplaces for the signs (1–6) Then write the job or jobs people do there. You have three minutes.**

Workplace	Jobs
1 hospital	*nurse, …*

2 ▶15 **Match the workplaces in the box to the signs (7–12). Listen and check. Then listen and repeat.**

gym ..... factory ..... garage .....
hair salon ..... office ..... travel agency .....

3 ▶16 **Work in pairs. Match the jobs to the descriptions. Then listen and check.**

1 An artist …
2 A cleaner …
3 A driver …
4 An engineer …
5 A fitness trainer …
6 A journalist …
7 A hairdresser …
8 A mechanic …
9 A pilot …
10 A dentist …
11 A secretary …
12 A travel agent …

a writes letters, organizes meetings, and makes phone calls.
b fixes cars when they're broken.
c cuts people's hair.
d writes articles for newspapers, websites, and TV.
e flies planes.
f fixes people's teeth.
g draws and paints pictures.
h drives people to different places.
i cleans rooms in buildings.
j helps people plan their vacations.
k helps people get strong and in shape.
l designs and builds machines, bridges, or roads.

4 **Who works at the places in Exercise 2?**

A fitness trainer works at a gym.

5 ▶17 PRONOUNCE **Listen to the words. Underline the consonants at the beginning of the words. Then listen again and repeat the words.**

bridge, cleaner, driver, flies, place, sports, student, strong, trainer

6 **Work in pairs. Student A thinks of a job. Student B asks questions to guess the job. Student A can only answer *yes* or *no*.**

Does this person work in an office?

No.

Does this person cut hair?

7 **THE MOVING PICTURE** **Watch the video and guess the job. Which job looks the hardest / the most exciting / the most boring / the most creative?**

SPEAK

8 **Tell your partner about the jobs of people you know, such as neighbors and family friends.**

MOVE BEYOND

Do the Words & Beyond exercise on page 66.

PHRASE BYTES

My neighbor's a …
My aunt works in …
My brother works as …
My father's friend helps the elderly …

Workbook, page 88

READING Dangerous jobs

»» Identify the topic

SPEAK AND READ

1 **Look at the photos. Would you like to do these jobs? Why or why not?**

2 **a** **Read the tips in the HOW TO box.**

b 18 **Read the numbered sections of a TV guide about two jobs. Each section is the beginning of a paragraph. Choose the topic that matches each section. There are two extra topics.**

a The dangers of the job
b Why he or she likes the job
c What you need for the job
d What the job is and what it's like
e The working hours

HOW TO

identify the topic

- ☐ The topic of a paragraph is usually in the first sentence. Read these "topic sentences" carefully.
- ☐ Identify important words in the topic sentences.

TODAY'S TV TIP:

The world's most dangerous jobs

ABOUT THE SHOW

This series looks at some of the world's most dangerous jobs. Pilots, war journalists, fishermen, even taxi drivers and construction engineers put their lives in danger every working day. In each show we'll follow two brave people with hard jobs.

ABOUT THIS SHOW

JAMES

1 Cleaning windows isn't an easy job. But for James, it can be a life or death task. James is an extreme window cleaner and cleans tall office buildings up to 30 floors high …

2 Not everyone can do this job. You don't have to be Spider-Man, but you can't be scared of heights. James had to have special training, and he uses a lot of safety equipment. He looks like a mountain climber, not a window cleaner …

3 Strong winds or rain can be very dangerous when you're on the outside of a skyscraper. James regularly checks the weather and his equipment. He knows that if he falls, he'll die. We follow him on a typical day …

MALEE

1 Training wild animals is never boring. Malee knows that – she's a crocodile trainer at a zoo in Thailand. Her job is to train crocodiles in shows for tourists …

2 Personality is important if you want to be an animal trainer. You must be patient – and very brave. Malee didn't have to take any exams for this job, but she has to know how crocodiles behave. She also has to know how to react quickly …

3 Every day Malee risks her life to entertain tourists. In the show she puts her arm in the mouth of a crocodile or lies with her head in its mouth. The crocodiles are four to five meters long, and their teeth are huge. Will Malee always be lucky?

3 **Which tips in the HOW TO box did you use for help with Exercise 2b? Check (✓) them.**

4 **Work in pairs.**

a **Student A reads the information about James again. Student B reads the information about Malee. Take notes on the topics in Exercise 2b.**

b **Tell your partner about James or Malee.**

PHRASE BYTES

I think they're brave because the animals are very dangerous / they risk …

I think they're cruel because crocodiles are wild animals / they might hurt …

Some people like danger / do it for the money / need a job.

I'd prefer …

REACT

5 **Work in pairs. What do you think? Tell your partner.**

1 Do you think animal trainers are brave or cruel? Why?
2 Why do people do dangerous jobs?
3 Would you prefer a safe job or a dangerous one? Why?

MOVE BEYOND

Put the jobs on page 16 in order from *dangerous* (1) to *not so dangerous* (12).

»» Workbook, page 89

GRAMMAR *Must* and *mustn't*, *have to* and *don't have to*

»» Talk about things you need or don't need to do

READ »» Grammar in context

1 Ella's class is doing a project on jobs. Read her description of her mom's work. What are her responsibilities?

What do your parents do? Does your mom or your dad have to do anything dangerous at work? My mom's a pilot. For her job she has to fly all over Australia. (Many people in Australia order things by plane, so they don't have to travel thousands of kilometers to the nearest town.)

One day, my mom had to land her plane in the ocean. Luckily she was unhurt and she didn't have to go to the hospital. "Were you scared?" I asked her. "No," she said. "In a difficult situation, you mustn't get scared. You must stay cool and do the job."

STUDY

2 Underline the words below in Exercise 1. Then complete the explanations.

have to	don't have to	must
has to	doesn't have to	mustn't
had to	didn't have to	

Have to, don't have to, must, mustn't

Which words mean …
it's necessary to do it? ________ , ________
it isn't necessary to do it? ________
it's forbidden to do it? ________

Affirmative
Use *have to*, *has to*, and *must* + ________ .
She has to fly all over Australia.

Negative
Use ________ or ________ + *have to* + base verb
My mom doesn't have to work in an office.
They don't have to travel thousands of kilometers.
Use *must* + ________ + base verb. What is the contraction? ________
You mustn't get scared.

Past
The past tense of *have to* is ________ .
The past tense of *don't have* is ________ .
For the past tense of *must*, use *had to*.

Questions and short answers
do, *does*, *did* + subject + *have* + base verb
________ *your Mom* ________ *to do anything dangerous at work?*
No, she doesn't.

See GRAMMAR DATABASE, page 61.

»» Workbook, pages 90–91

PRACTICE

3 Complete Ella's interview with her mom. Use the correct *have to* form of the verbs.

Ella: (1) *Do you have to work* (you / work) long hours?
Mom: Yes, I work 10–12 hours on some days. But I (2) ________ (not work) every day.
Ella: What training (3) ________ (a pilot / do)?
Mom: Well, a pilot (4) ________ (take) flying lessons, of course.
Ella: (5) ________ (you / take) an exam before you got the job?
Mom: Yes, we (6) ________ (take) a lot of exams before we could become pilots.
Ella: Can I ask one more question or (7) ________ (you / go) now?
Mom: Sorry, (8) I ________ (start) work soon.

4 Complete the sentences with *must* or *mustn't*.

1 Doctors *must* have clean hands.
2 Teachers ________ shout at their students.
3 Mechanics ________ know about cars.
4 Drivers ________ drive too fast.
5 Engineers ________ make mistakes.
6 Journalists ________ write true stories.

5 Choose the correct options.

I'm a hairdresser. I (1) *mustn't* / *don't have to* start work early, but I (2) *have to* / *don't have to* work long hours. In the salon I (3) *have to* / *don't have to* wash and cut people's hair. I (4) *must* / *mustn't* be on time and I (5) *have to* / *mustn't* be unfriendly or rude. The customers (6) *must* / *don't have to* be happy when they leave.

6 Write the questions with *have to*.

1 anybody in your family / work / long hours?
Does anybody in your family have to work long hours?
2 anybody in your family / work with customers / in his or her job?
____
3 you / work / hard at school?
____
4 you / do a lot of homework?
____
5 you / do chores at home?
____

SPEAK

7 Work in pairs. Ask and answer the questions in Exercise 6.

Recognize a speaker's message

SPEAK AND LISTEN

1 Read Paige Rohrick's online profile. Then answer the questions.

1 How old is she?
2 Where does she live?
3 What's her main interest?
4 What other things does she like?

ABOUT PAIGE

INTERVIEW

My name is Paige Rohrick. I'm 17 years old and I'm from Vancouver, Canada. I love to draw and share my ideas with others. Over the years I have tried a lot of drawing styles, and manga is my favorite style now. My other interests include designing clothes and cooking. I recently competed in a competition for dress design in Vancouver. My dress came in second!

2 ▶19 Now listen to an interview with Paige. Complete the notes with one word or number.

Paige's apps

PaigeeDraw	helps people learn how to draw (1) *manga* .
ChibiDraw	helps people become more (2) .... at drawing.
PaigeeDraw Boys	helps people draw (3) ....

PaigeeDraw

Had idea	when she was (4) .... years old.
App development	(5) .... years.
Help from	father, mother, and (6) ....
Number of downloads	(7) ....

Work and study

School	Still in (8) .... school.
Career plan	get into a good college / (9) .... school.
	Wants to be a fashion (10) ....

HOW TO recognize a speaker's message

☐ Listen for phrases like *My advice / tip is …*
☐ Listen for imperatives, *can / can't*, and *should / shouldn't*.
☐ Listen for the words the speaker emphasizes.

3 a Read the tips in the HOW TO box.

b ▶19 Listen again. What's Paige's message? Choose A, B, or C.

A Make your own app – it's easy!
B It isn't easy, but you can do it!
C Think about your future career now!

4 Which tips in the HOW TO box did you use for help with Exercise 3b? Check (✓) them.

WORK WITH WORDS

5 ▶20 Listen and read the information about Paige. Underline the words in bold about work. Circle the words in bold about study.

Paige sees her future (a) **career** in art and design. She has her own (b) **company** and she's good at (c) **business**, but she thinks it's important to get a (d) **degree**. She plans to take art (e) **classes** in (f) **college**. First she has to finish high school and pass her (g) **exams**. Her website PaigeeDraw isn't just a (h) **part-time job** – it's a (i) **full-time job**. This means she's very busy during the school (j) **semester** with study and work.

6 a ▶21 Listen to the definitions and write the correct letter from Exercise 5 for each one.

1 *d* 3 ___ 5 ___ 7 ___ 9 ___
2 ___ 4 ___ 6 ___ 8 ___ 10 ___

b ▶22 Listen and check your answers.

REACT

7 Work in pairs. Ask and answer the questions. Explain your answers.

1 Would you like to have your own company? Why or why not?
2 Do you think a college degree is important? Why or why not?
3 Do you plan to go to college?

MOVE BEYOND

Do the Words & Beyond exercise on page 66.

Workbook, pages 92–93

GRAMMAR Present perfect

Talk about actions and events at a nonspecific time in the past

READ Grammar in context

1 Read about another teen app designer. Why is it hard to get help designing apps?

Many teenagers **have designed** apps, but Thomas Suarez from California **has become** one of the world's youngest app developers – he's 12. Thomas **has developed** two successful apps, and he'**s started** an app club at school too. With his help, other kids **have made** their own apps. As Thomas **has said**, it's hard to get help with this. Many parents **have been to** sports classes or **have played** a musical instrument, but most parents **haven't written** apps. (**Have** you or your parents **done** this?)

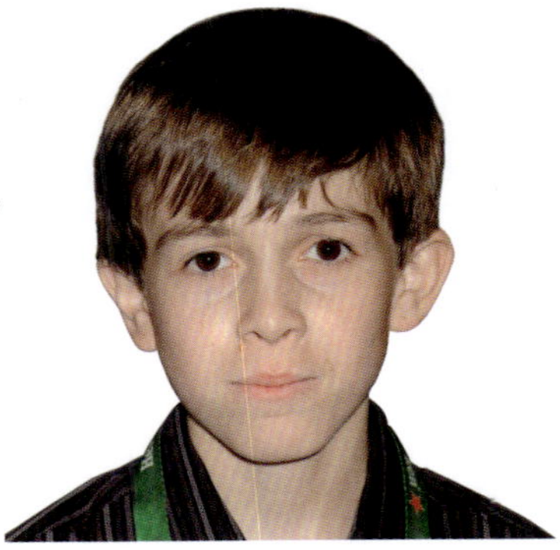

STUDY

2 The verbs in bold in Exercise 1 are in the present perfect tense. Complete the explanations.

Present perfect

Use the present perfect for actions in the past when you don't know the exact time they happened.

Affirmative sentences use ________ or ________ + past participle.

Many teenagers have designed apps.
Thomas has developed two successful apps.

Negative sentences use ________ or ________ + past participle.

Most parents haven't written apps.

Questions use ________ or ________ + subject + past participle.

Have you or your parents done this?

Regular past participles add *-ed* to the verb.

See GRAMMAR DATABASE, page 61.

See IRREGULAR VERBS, page 70.

3 Underline six irregular past participles in Exercise 1. Which verbs are they from?

4 Choose the correct option.

Been to or gone to

The students have been to the app club. They really enjoyed it.
They are **still at the club / not at the club.**
The students have gone to the app club. They're designing a new app.
They are **still at the club / not at the club.**

See GRAMMAR DATABASE, page 61.

PRACTICE

5 Complete the sentences with the past participle forms of the verbs in the box. (Use page 140 for help with irregular verbs.)

be decide give plan ~~share~~ speak start tell

1 Thomas Suarez has *shared* his skills with others.
2 He has ________ at important conferences.
3 He has ________ speeches about his app club.
4 He has ________ about using apps in schools.
5 His club has ________ to develop apps for tablets in schools.
6 Teachers and students in schools have ________ Thomas what apps they need.
7 Thomas has ________ a lot of projects for the future.
8 He has ________ his own company.

6 Complete the text about a teen businessman with the correct form of the verbs.

Farrhad Acidwalla from Mumbai, India, is only 18 but (1) he *'s achieved* (**achieve**) more than other 18-year-olds. Farrhad (2) ________ (**build**) a communications company from nothing, and now 42 people work for him. How (3) ________ (**he / do**) it? His parents (4) ________ (**support**) him all the way, but it (5) ________ (**not be**) easy. He (6) ________ (**made**) mistakes. Farrhad says that his success (7) ________ (**not change**) him, but his mistakes (8) ________ (**teach**) him many important things.

WRITE AND SPEAK

7 a Write six things you have or haven't done. Use the verbs in the box or your own ideas.

be design help make play win write

b Work in pairs. Ask and answer questions about what you have or haven't done.

I've written an article for a website. Have you written an article?

Yes, I have. I haven't designed an app. Have you designed an app?

No, I haven't, but I've ...

Workbook, page 94

LANGUAGE & BEYOND

Questionnaire about time	Josh, USA	Luiza, Brazil
1 What time do you start school?	7:45 a.m.	7:00 a.m.
2 What time do you have lunch? How long is lunchtime?	11:30 a.m. (30 minutes)	1:00 p.m. (45 minutes)
3 Do stores close at lunchtime?	No	No
4 When do you finish school?	2:45 p.m.	12:00 p.m.
5 What time do you have dinner?	6:30 p.m.	8:00 p.m.
6 You're meeting a friend at home or in a café, or visit friends or family for dinner. When do you arrive?	On time	30–60 minutes late
7 How do you feel when you have to wait?	I hate waiting.	It's no problem.

»» Understand how different cultures think about time

RESPECT OTHERS

READ

1 Read the questionnaire and the answers from two students. What differences do you notice in the answers?

DO

2 Complete the questionnaire for you. Compare your answers with a partner. Then compare your answers with Josh's and Luiza's answers. What's the same? What's different?

3 Read what Josh said to a friend. Why do you think both families were a little unhappy?

Last night Dad's friend and his wife came to our house. He's from Brazil. Dad said seven o'clock and the food was all ready, but they came at eight o'clock. We were all really hungry! They were a little surprised when we ate soon after. We finished very quickly. And they didn't seem very happy when Mom went to bed after dessert!

REFLECT

4 Discuss the questions with your class. Do you agree with the REFLECTION POINT?

1 How much time do you spend at the table at mealtimes?
2 Which is more important for you: spending time with family and friends or doing homework and chores?
3 In what situations is it OK or not OK to be late in your country?

EXTEND

5 Work in pairs or a small group. Write some tips for visitors to your country. Include tips about time: when things happen and what visitors should or shouldn't do.

REFLECTION POINT

In different cultures, people do things at different times and think about time in different ways. When you're in a different country or meet people from different countries, try to understand their time system.

PHRASE BYTES

In my country, people usually …
It's important to (spend a lot of time on) …
It isn't important to …
You should / have to …
You shouldn't / mustn't …

»» Workbook, page 97

SPEAKING Sorry!

Make and react to apologies

SPEAK

1 **Discuss what's happening in the picture.**

2 **Read these excuses. Which one do you think is the best? What other good excuses do you know?**

Excuse Generator

When you haven't done homework

- I was doing it on the bus to school and it blew out the window.
- I put it in my jacket and my mom washed it.
- I left it in the car and my dad took the car to the garage.

When you're late for school

- I lost my glasses and got on the wrong bus.
- I couldn't remember the way.
- It's really foggy outside and I couldn't find the school.

LISTEN

3 23 **Listen to the conversations. In which conversations (1–6) does somebody accept the other person's apology (say it's OK)?**

1 **Amy:** I haven't done my homework. I'm really sorry, but we had an important basketball game yesterday.
Teacher: That's (a) ________ . You can do it for tomorrow.

2 **Barbara:** Sorry I'm late. I had to go to the doctor.
Teacher: That's (b) ________ . Sit down.

3 **Joe:** Sorry I'm late. I missed the bus. I think the bus driver came early.
Teacher: That's not (c) ________ enough. You should get up earlier.

4 **Ken:** I forgot your DVD. I'm really sorry. I'll bring it tomorrow.
José: Don't (d) ________ about it. Tomorrow's fine.

5 **Nancy:** Um, I lost the paper with the information for our project. I'm sorry. I've looked everywhere for it.
Gustavo: (e) ________ we need it for history class. What are we going to do?

6 **Jen:** Sorry I didn't call you yesterday. I forgot to charge my phone.
Rosa: That's OK, no (f) ________ .

4 23 **Listen again and complete the conversations with the words in the box. Which phrases do you use when you DON'T accept an apology?**

all right but good OK problem worry

ACT

5 **You're going to make apologies for the situations below.**
- **First think of good explanations or excuses.**
- **Work in pairs. Make apologies and react to your partner's apologies.**

1 You're late for school.
2 You haven't done your homework.
3 You've forgotten or lost something of your partner's.

PHRASEBOOK 24

Make an apology

I'm (really) sorry.
Sorry I'm late.
Sorry, I forgot / lost …
I had to …

Accept / refuse an apology

✓ That's OK. / That's all right.
✓ Don't worry about it.
✓ No problem. / Never mind.
✗ That's not good enough.
✗ But …

Workbook, page 95

WRITING My chores

Start and finish informal emails and letters

SPEAK AND READ

1 Read Daniel's email. What chores does he have to do?

Hi, Milos,

How are you? Sorry I haven't written for a while. I've been really busy with things at school. In your last email, you asked me what chores I have to do. I have to make my bed every day and clean my room on the weekend. I also have to help wash the dishes after dinner. I don't have to cook, but I like helping my mom when she makes pancakes. I also have to take out the garbage. We've started to sort things for recycling so now that's my job too! What chores do you have to do?

I have to run. It's time for soccer practice. Write soon!

Daniel

2 a Read the tips in the HOW TO box.

HOW TO

start and finish informal emails and letters

- **Start** *Thanks for your email / letter.*
  How are you?
  Sorry I haven't written for a while.
- **Finish** *I have to run.*
  Write soon!
  See you soon!

b Which of the phrases does Daniel use? Underline them in his email.

PRACTICE

3 Complete parts of six emails with the correct phrases from the HOW TO box.

Start

1 *Sorry I haven't written for a while.* I've been really busy.

2 .... It's great to hear from you.

3 .... I'm OK, but I'm a little tired.

Finish

4 .... I want to read all your news!

5 .... We can talk then.

6 .... I have a piano lesson now.

DISCUSS

4 Discuss your chores and if you like to do them or not.

WRITE

5 Write an email to Milos about the chores you have to do.

1 Write six sentences about your chores. Use *have to*, *don't have to*, *must*, *mustn't* to explain your responsibilities.

2 Explain how you feel about the chore. Is it easy, fun, enjoyable, or boring?

3 Start and finish your email with an informal phrase. See the HOW TO box.

SHARE

6 Read your email to your classmates. Who has a lot of responsibilities at home? Do the boys have different responsibilities than the girls?

Workbook, pages 96–97

VOCABULARY Jobs and workplaces

1 Complete the website with the correct jobs.

It's good to think about job choices now – even if you still have years of school left. Check out these job links!

- Do you think it's important to look good? A job as a (1) h__________ might be for you.
- Good at organizing things? How about a job in an office as a (2) s__________?
- Do you think healthy teeth are important? A (3) d__________ sounds like the job for you.
- Are you good at sports? Then you might like to be a (4) f__________ t__________.
- Interested in machines and how things work? How about a job as an (5) e__________?
- Good with words? You may like a job as a (6) j__________ with a magazine.
- Do you like travel? Think about a job as a (7) p__________ or a (8) t__________ a__________.
- If you enjoy drawing and painting, you might like to be an (9) a__________.
- Do you like cars? Then a job as a (10) d__________ or as a (11) m__________ is right for you.
- Good at keeping things neat and clean? How about being a (12) c__________?

___ /12

Work and study

2 Complete the description with the words from the box.

business career company class exams full-time job part-time job degrees year college

Dangerous Jobs Agency: School Cleaner

A school cleaner may work for one school, or he or she may work for a cleaning (1) __________ and work for several different schools. It can be a (2) __________ for a few hours or a (3) __________. Most of the work is during the school (4) __________.

You can get a cleaning job when you've finished school and taken your (5) __________. To get into the school cleaning 6) __________, you can't be afraid of dirt! You don't need any special (7) __________ and you don't need to go to (8) __________, but you can take a short (9) __________ in cleaning. Do you want to make school cleaning your (10) __________? Good luck!

___ /10

GRAMMAR *Must* and *mustn't*, *have to* and *don't have to*

3 Choose the correct options.

Dangerous Jobs Agency
Dangerous job tips: School secretary

1 You *have to* / *don't have to* speak three languages.
2 You *must* / *mustn't* know a lot about student excuses.
3 You *has to* / *have to* be organized.
4 You *don't have to* / *mustn't* be scared of angry parents.
5 You *must* / *don't have to* know how to use a computer.
6 You *don't have to* / *mustn't* work long hours (luckily!).

___ /12

Present perfect

4 Complete the conversation with the present perfect form of the verbs.

A: Welcome to the Dangerous Jobs Agency! (1) __________ (you / decide) on a career?
B: No, I (2) __________. But I (3) __________ (read) the tips on your website. I don't want to be a school secretary or cleaner. Those jobs are much too dangerous!
A: Well, (4) __________ (you / see) the information about a wild animal trainer?
B: Hm, I (5) __________ (not / think) about a job with animals. But it sounds interesting.
A: A job for an assistant trainer (6) __________ (become) available at the zoo. (7) __________ (you / have) experience with wild animals?
B: I have a fish. But it (8) __________ (not / learn) to do any tricks.

___ /16

Your score: ___ /50

SKILLS CHECK

✓✓✓ Yes, I can. No problem!
✓✓ Yes, I can. But I need a little help.
✓ Yes, I can. But I need a lot of help.

I can identify the topic of paragraphs when I read. ______
I can recognize a speaker's message. ______
I can understand different ways to see time. ______
I can make and react to apologies. ______
I can start and finish informal emails and letters. ______

Workbook, pages 98–99

UNIT 8

MEDIA MIX

IN THE PICTURE What's on?

»» Talk about movies and TV shows

WORK WITH WORDS

1 a RECALL **Work in pairs. Write the words in the correct columns. Can you add any other words? You have three minutes.**

a CD   a comic book   a DVD   a magazine   a movie   music
a newspaper   a podcast   a TV show   a video   a website

Watch	Read	Listen to
television	*a book*	*the radio*

b **Work in pairs. Talk about the things from Exercise 1 you like and don't like doing.**

2 25 **Match the TV shows and movies to the photos. Listen and check. Then listen and repeat.**

action/adventure *i*   cartoon ___   talk show ___   comedy ___
cooking show ___   documentary ___   game show ___   horror ___
news ___   science fiction ___   weather ___   western ___

PHRASE BYTES

I like reading books.
I really enjoy watching television.
I don't like …

3 **Which things in Exercise 2 can you only see on television and not at the movie theater?**

4 26 **Complete the conversation with words from Exercise 2. Then listen and check.**

Mike: Did you see the baseball score on the (1) *news* ?
Jess: No, I was watching that new (2) ________ show. It was really funny.
Mike: There's a (3) ________ movie on later called *Tower of Terror*. Do you want to see it?
Jess: No. If I watch it, I'll have bad dreams and I won't sleep.
Mike: How about a (4) ________ ? You like horses and cowboys.
Jess: No, thanks. There's an interesting nature (5) ________ about wild animals.
Mike: OK. But first can we watch the *Be My Guest* (6) ________ ? Sometimes the interviews are really good.

5 THE MOVING PICTURE 27 **Watch the video. How many kinds of shows and movies can you identify?**

6 **a** ▶28 PRONOUNCE **Listen to the word. Underline the /ʧ/ sound.**

watch

b ▶29 **Listen and underline the /ʧ/ sound in the words. Then listen again and repeat the words.**

chair much nature share show wash which

SPEAK

7 **Work in pairs. Do a TV and movie survey. Student A asks the questions on page 71. Student B asks the questions on page 72. Then compare your answers with the rest of the class.**

MOVE BEYOND

Do the Words & Beyond exercise on page 67.

Workbook, page 92

READING A long time ago ...

Identify the author's argument

SPEAK AND READ

1 Work in pairs. Look at the photos and answer the questions.

1 What kinds of movies can you see in the photos?
2 Which of the movies do you recognize?
3 What are the titles of the movies?

2 a Read the tips in the HOW TO box.

b 30 **Read the article and answer the questions.**

1 What is the author's main argument?
2 How many reasons does he give to support the argument?
3 Which is the most important reason in the author's opinion?

HOW TO
identify the author's argument

- ☐ Look for the author's opinion near the beginning of the text.
- ☐ Then find reasons: look for words / phrases like *first*, *second*, *for example*.
- ☐ Look for a summary at the end of the text.

STAR WARS (1977)

121 min | Action & Adventure | Science Fiction

Your **rating**: ★★★★★

Summary: A young Luke Skywalker tries to rescue Princess Leia from the evil Darth Vader and save the galaxy from the dangerous Empire.
Director: George Lucas
Stars: Mark Hamill, Harrison Ford, and Carrie Fisher

A long time ago in a galaxy far, far away, a movie called *Star Wars* opened and became one of the most important movies in history.

There has never been a movie like *Star Wars*. The movie's **characters** have become universal symbols of good and bad. Phrases like "May the Force be with you" have entered the English language, and it has had a huge influence on other movies.

There are several reasons for the movie's importance. First, it used different **genres** in one movie. *Star Wars* was a science fiction movie, but it was also an adventure movie. Many of the movie's ideas also came from westerns. Second, it was one of the first movies to use computer-generated special effects successfully. Third, it was one of the first big summer movies.

Today we call big, expensive, successful movies "**blockbusters**." Most blockbusters arrive in theaters between the months of May and September. For example, the *Pirates of the Caribbean*, *Spider-Man*, and *Transformers* movies were all summer blockbusters.

Finally, *Star Wars* was the first movie to produce **merchandise**. Apart from the six movies and the TV series, there have also been *Star Wars* books, comic books, magazines, DVDs, action figures, board games, video games, T-shirts, and cups.

For all of these reasons, especially the last one, I believe *Star Wars* changed movies forever. Have *you* ever seen the original *Star Wars* movie? If you have, then I'm sure you'll agree with me.

3 Which tips in the HOW TO box did you use for help with Exercise 2b? Check (✓) them.

4 Read all the text above again. Match the words in green to the definitions.

1 Popular movies *blockbusters*
2 Kinds of movies ....
3 A measurement of something's popularity ....
4 A short version with the most important details ....
5 People in a book or movie ....
6 Something people buy and sell ....

REACT

5 Work in pairs. Ask and answer the questions.

1 Which *Star Wars* movies have you seen?
2 What's your favorite science fiction movie? Why do you like it?
3 What other blockbuster movies have you seen?

MOVE BEYOND

Choose another blockbuster movie. How much do you know about the movie? Look at the first part of the information for *Star Wars* and make a note of the same information for your movie.

Workbook, page 101

GRAMMAR Present perfect with *ever* and *never*

>>> Talk about experiences

READ >>> Grammar in context

1 Read about the show *I've Never Seen Star Wars*. Is it a game show or a talk show?

I've Never Seen Star Wars is the title of a radio and television show. In each episode, a guest talks about, and tries doing, things that he or she has never done, like reading a famous book or listening to a kind of music. Have you ever listened to hip-hop? Have you ever read a *Harry Potter* book? These are examples of the things the show's guests have never done.

STUDY

2 Choose the correct options. Use Exercise 1 to help you.

Present perfect with *ever* or *never*

Use *ever* and *never* to talk about experiences you had or didn't have at any time in the past.

Ever* / *Never is used to ask if you did something at any time in the past.
*Have you **ever** / **never** seen Star Wars?*

Ever* / *Never is used to say you didn't do something at any time in the past.
*I've **ever** / **never** seen Star Wars.*

Ever and *never* go **before** / **after** the past participle.
Has he ever listened to hip hop?
She has never been to Patagonia.

Give a short answer with *have, has, haven't, hasn't*.
*Yes, he **have** / **has**.*
*No, I **haven't** / **hasn't**.*

See GRAMMAR DATABASE, page 62.

PRACTICE

3 Complete the conversation.

Lily: Have you (1) *ever* seen *Star Wars*?
Omar: Yes, I (2) ______ . What about you?
Lily: No, I (3) ______ .
Omar: Have you (4) ______ watched *Ugly Betty*?
Lily: The TV series? No, I've (5) ______ watched it. Is it good?
Omar: I don't know. I've (6) ______ watched it either. It's about a personal assistant at a fashion magazine. She's not very pretty, but she's smart and funny.

Ugly Betty TV Series, 2006–2010, USA, 2008 Season 03, America Ferrera.

4 a Write questions about Lily and Omar. Then answer them. Use *never* in negative answers.

Lily / "Star Wars"
Has Lily ever seen "Star Wars"? No, she hasn't. She's never seen "Star Wars."

	Lily	Omar
Star Wars	✗	✓
Ugly Betty	✗	✗
Pirates of the Caribbean	✓	✗
The Simpsons	✓	✓
Transformers	✗	✓

1 Omar / *Star Wars*
2 Lily and Omar / *Ugly Betty*
3 Omar / *Pirates of the Caribbean*
4 Lily and Omar / *The Simpsons*
5 Lily / *Transformers*
6 Omar / *Transformers*

b Work in pairs. Student A reads out a question and Student B reads out the answer. Then change roles for the next question.

5 Write complete questions using *ever*.

1 cook a meal
Have you ever cooked a meal?
2 iron a shirt
______
3 eat with chopsticks
______
4 have a judo lesson
______
5 listen to hip-hop
______
6 play the piano
______

6 Work in pairs. Take turns asking and answering the questions in Exercise 5.

SPEAK

7 a Work in pairs. Think of more questions to ask your partner and find three things your partner has never done (using different verbs).

Have you ever sung karaoke?

No, I haven't.

b Imagine your partner is a guest on *I've Never Seen Star Wars*. Tell the class about the three things he or she has never done.

My guest has never sung karaoke.

LISTENING AND VOCABULARY My radio

Use the audio type to help you understand

SPEAK AND LISTEN

1 Work in pairs. Answer the questions.

1 How often do you listen to the radio?
2 What stations do you listen to?
3 Do you listen to the news on the radio? Why or why not?

PHRASE BYTES

I sometimes listen to …
The radio is usually on in / at …
I listen to the news because …

2 a Read the tips in the HOW TO box.

b 31 Listen. What's the audio type?

c 32 Listen and put the topics in the correct order (1–5).

___ Weather	___ Sports	___ Entertainment news
___ Top story	___ Traffic	

HOW TO

use the audio type to help you understand

- ☐ Identify the audio type. Is it a conversation? A speech? A news program?
- ☐ Think about the type of information you might hear.
- ☐ Listen for words and phrases you expect to hear.

3 Which tips in the HOW TO box did you use for help with Exercises 2b and 2c? Check (✓) them.

4 33 Listen again. Choose the right answer (A, B, or C).

1 What's the top story about?
A street crime B a soccer game C traffic problems
2 When's the soccer game in Rio de Janeiro?
A this afternoon B tonight C tomorrow
3 What kind of movie has Dario Stone made?
A a comedy B an action movie C a documentary
4 Where are the traffic problems?
A on the highway B in Rio de Janeiro C on Main Street
5 What's the weather like?
A rainy and windy B windy and cloudy C sunny

1

2

3

4

WORK WITH WORDS

5 34 Match the crime words to the pictures. Listen and check. Then listen and repeat.

accident ambulance arrest (v) ~~crime~~ criminal
police car police officer steal (v) thief victim

1 *crime*, ______, ______, ______
2 ______, ______, ______
3 ______, ______
4 ______

6 35 Complete the sentences with the correct form of the words from Exercise 5. Then listen and check.

1 The ______ was walking out of a department store when a ______ ran up and ______ her purse.
2 The atmosphere is friendly, but ______ have already ______ three people.
3 Dario Stone's new action movie is about an extremely dangerous ______.
4 There's been a(n) ______ on Main Street. Several ______ and a(n) ______ are at the scene.

7 Read the sentences in Exercise 6 out loud in the style of the news reporters.

REACT

8 Work in pairs. What do you think? Tell your partner.

1 Which sections of news programs do you like and not like? Why?
2 What stories are in the news right now?

MOVE BEYOND

Do the Words & Beyond exercise on page 67.

Workbook, pages 104–105

GRAMMAR Present perfect with *already*, *yet*, and *just*

Talk about things related to the present

READ AND LISTEN Grammar in context

1 36 **Read and listen to the conversation. What's missing? Who wanted to look at it?**

Harry: Where's Mike? It's one o'clock and he hasn't arrived **yet**.
Marta: I don't know. I've **just** come back from lunch. Why?
Harry: Someone's stolen my phone. I think it was Mike.
Marta: I saw it in the classroom before I went to lunch. I'll go and …
Harry: I've **already** looked there. Mike wanted to look at it. Now it's gone!
Marta: Have you told anyone else **yet**?

STUDY

2 Choose the correct options. Use Exercise 1 to help you.

Present perfect with *already*, *yet*, and *just*

For very recent actions, use *just*.
For actions completed before now, use *already*.
To ask if an action is completed or not, use *yet*.
To say an action isn't completed, use *yet*.

Put *just* and *already* ***before*** / ***after*** the past participle in affirmative sentences.
I've just called the police.
They've already responded.

Put *yet* at the ***beginning*** / ***end*** of negative sentences and questions.
I haven't called the police yet.

Note: *Already*, *just*, and *yet* are used with the present perfect tense. Notice that a specific time isn't mentioned. The simple past tense is used when a specific time is mentioned.

See GRAMMAR DATABASE, page 62.

PRACTICE

3 Complete the phone conversation between Marta and Mike with *already*, *just*, or *yet*.

Marta: Mike. It's Marta. I've (1) *just* seen Harry.
Mike: Has he noticed the missing phone (2) ________?
Marta: Yes. He's (3) ________ looked in the classroom. He thinks you're a thief.
Mike: I've never stolen anything, Marta. I broke it. That's all.
Marta: Where are you?
Mike: I've (4) ________ gotten home. I'm trying to fix it.
Marta: No. Don't do that. You've (5) ________ caused enough problems.
Mike: So what should I do?
Marta: He hasn't told anyone (6) ________. I think you should come back and tell him the truth.

4 It's one o'clock. Write sentences using *just*, *already*, and *yet*.

1 Marta / have / lunch.
Marta has just had lunch.
2 Mike / break / the phone.
____
3 Harry / look / in the classroom.
____
4 Marta / call / Mike.
____
5 Mike / fix / the phone.
____

5 Complete the four situations with the present perfect or simple past form of the verbs.

1 A friend (1) *asked* (ask) you for some money two weeks ago, but he/she (2) ________ (not return) it yet.
2 You're in a shopping mall and you (3) ________ (just / see) someone steal some batteries from a shop.
3 Yesterday you (4) ________ (tell) your best friend a secret. You (5) ________ (just / discover) that he/she (6) ________ (already / tell) some of your classmates.
4 You (7) ________ (just / see) an accident on the street. A woman was crossing the street when a car (8) ________ (hit) her.

SPEAK

6 Work in pairs. Role-play the situations in Exercise 5.

You haven't returned my money yet.

I'm sorry I haven't paid you back. How about next week?

Workbook, page 106

LANGUAGE & BEYOND

>>> Talk about problems

COMMUNICATE & COOPERATE

SPEAK AND READ

1 Work in pairs. Look at the photo. What's the situation?

2 37 Read and listen to the script from a TV show. What kind of show is it? Explain your answer.

Episode 19, scene 1: At home, Mom is late for work.
Mia: Mom? Can I talk to you?
Mom: Now isn't a good time, dear.
Mia: (angry) It's never a good time. You're always busy.
Mom: What do you want to talk about?
Mia: (walking away) Nothing. It isn't important.

Episode 19, scene 2: In the park, Mia is with Dad.
Mia: Dad? I need your advice. Can we talk?
Dad: Of course. What's the problem?
Mia: A friend at school has asked me to lie for her.
Dad: Why? What has she done?
Mia: She's not going to school and she doesn't want her parents to find out.

3 Work in pairs. Answer the questions.

1 What does Mia want to talk about? Why?
2 Who does she talk to?
3 Which conversation helps Mia feel better? Why?

PHRASE BYTES

She wants to talk about …

I think Mia feels better when she talks to …

DO

4 Work in groups. Look at the tips for talking with parents and choose the correct option.

1 Talk when your parents *are* / *aren't* busy.
2 *Explain* / *Don't explain* what you need or want (help or advice).
3 Try *to* / *not to* argue.
4 *Tell them* / *Don't tell them* the truth.

5 Look at the scenes in Exercise 2. Which tips from Exercise 4 does Mia follow or not follow? Check (✓) them.

REFLECTION POINT

It's best to talk about problems, not avoid them. People can only help you if they understand your problem. Find the right time and place to talk.

REFLECT

6 Discuss the questions with your class. Do you agree with the REFLECTION POINT?

1 Why is it good to talk about problems?
2 What happens if you don't talk about problems?
3 Do you think the tips in Exercise 4 are good? Can you think of any more tips?

EXTEND

7 Work in groups. Think of another situation in which Mia could talk to both her parents about the problem in Exercise 2. Write the scene and then present it to the class.

Workbook, page 109

SPEAKING I know what you mean, but ...

»» Agree and disagree with someone

SPEAK

1 Work in pairs. Answer the questions.

1 What was the last movie you saw at the movie theater or on TV?
2 Who did you see it with?
3 What did you think of the movie? Did the other people agree with you?

LISTEN

2 ▶38 Listen to the conversation. Who enjoyed the movie more – Frank or Gina?

Frank: So what did you think of the movie?
Gina: I liked it, but it was a little slow.
Frank: I know what you mean, but I thought the ending was amazing.
Gina: Yes, but what about the rest of it? The story wasn't very real.
Frank: I don't agree. I thought it was real.
Gina: And the acting was terrible.
Frank: You're right. The acting was bad, but the movie was funny.
Gina: I agree, but it was only funny 'cause it was so bad.
Frank: I totally disagree.
Gina: You're wrong.
Frank: Maybe, but I really liked it.
Gina: I liked it too, but it was just so-so.

3 ▶38 Listen again. Which things do Frank and Gina agree on?

4 ▶39 Complete the phrases from the conversation. Then listen and repeat.

✓	✗
You're right. I *agree* . I know what you ________ .	You're wrong. I totally ________ . I don't ________ .

5 ▶40 Complete the sentences with one word. Listen and check. Then listen and repeat.

1 The movie was good, ________ the acting was terrible.
2 You're right, ________ I really liked it.

6 ▶41 Think of a movie you've seen recently. Listen to Frank. Do you agree with him? Listen and respond with a phrase from Exercise 4.

ACT

7 In groups of three or four, complete the tasks.

1 Choose a movie you've all seen.
2 You've just watched the movie together. What did you all think of it?

PHRASEBOOK ▶42

Asking for and giving opinions

What did you think of ... ?
Did you like ... ?
What about ... ?
I thought ... was / were ...
I liked ... / I didn't like ...

Agreeing and disagreeing

You're right / wrong.
I agree. / I don't agree. / I disagree.
I know what you mean, (but ...)
I totally agree / disagree.

»» Workbook, page 99

WRITING The best movie ever

Give opinions

SPEAK AND READD

1 Work in pairs. Look at the pictures and answer the questions.

1 Have you seen any of the movies or TV series?
2 Do you know the names of any of the characters?
3 What do the movies and TV series have in common?

PHRASE BYTES

This is a scene from …
… is a character in …
I think they're all …

2 Read Sara's movie review and answer her question.

THE BEST MOVIE I'VE EVER SEEN

The best movie I've ever seen is *Toy Story 3*. It's an adventure film, a comedy, and a cartoon. When Andy leaves home to go to college, he gives his toys to a day-care center. The toys then plan an escape. I like this movie because of the characters. Woody, Buzz, and all the other toys are like my friends. Personally, I love the way the film combines comedy, action, and horror. In my opinion, the best part is Buzz speaking Spanish. In my view, *Toy Story 3* is about real life. We all grow up, but our toys don't. For all these reasons (and many more), *Toy Story 3* is the best movie I've ever seen. What's the best movie you've ever seen?

3 a Read the tips in the HOW TO box.

HOW TO
give opinions

- Use phrases like *In my opinion, Personally, In my view …*
- Give reasons for your opinions. *I like this movie because …*
- Give an example of something you like a lot. Add details.

b Underline the opinion phrases in Sara's review. What example does she give?

PRACTICE

4 Use the words in the HOW TO box to complete this review.

The best movie I've ever seen is *Stand By Me*. It's an adventure film about four 12-year-old boys. They go on a journey to find another boy – the victim of an accident. (1) ________ because it's really funny, exciting, and sad at the same time. (2) ________ opinion, the actors are fantastic, especially River Phoenix. (3) ________ , I think the best scene is on the rail bridge. The four friends have to cross the bridge before the train comes. It's amazing! It's an old movie, but in (4) ________ it doesn't feel old. It's about important themes – friends and growing up. If you watch *Stand By Me*, I know you'll enjoy it.

DISCUSS

5 Discuss a movie you like and explain why you like it.

WRITE

6 Write a movie review about a movie you like or don't like.

1 First, say what kind of movie it is (for example, romance, action, or western). Then summarize what happened in the movie. Describe one or two characters.
2 Use opinion phrases to talk about your favorite part or characters. See the HOW TO box.
3 Use the present perfect with *ever, never, already,* or *yet*. Tell your readers how many times you have seen this movie. Ask your readers if they've seen the movie yet.

SHARE

7 Present your review to a small group or your class. Which movies have you already seen? Do you agree with the review? Which movies would you like to see?

Workbook, pages 108–109

VOCABULARY Kinds of movies and TV shows

1 Complete the words.

1 a _ _ _ _ n / a _ _ _ _ _ _ _ e
2 c _ _ _ _ _ n
3 t _ _ k s _ _ w
4 c _ _ _ _ y
5 c _ _ _ _ _ g s _ _ w
6 d _ _ _ _ _ _ _ _ _ y
7 g _ _ e s _ _ w
8 h _ _ _ _ r
9 n _ _ s
10 s _ _ _ _ _ e f _ _ _ _ _ n
11 w _ _ _ _ _ r
12 w _ _ _ _ _ n

___ /12

Crime

2 Complete the description with the correct form of the words in the box.

accident ambulance arrest crime criminal police car police officer steal thief victim

Today's movie choice is the police drama *Too Much Crime in the City*. In this exciting movie, Rob Taylor plays the part of a(n) (1) ________ at a New York police station. One day a(n) (2) ________ (3) ________ some money from a woman in the street. He doesn't know, but the (4) ________ of the (5) ________ is Taylor's girlfriend. Taylor follows the (6) ________ in a (7) ________ and (8) ________ him. But on the way back to the station, there's a car (9) ________. Taylor needs a(n) (10) ________ and he needs it fast!

___ /10

GRAMMAR Present perfect with *ever* and *never*

3 Complete the interview with the present perfect form of the verbs.

Reporter: (1) ________ (you / ever / play) the part of a police officer before?
Rob Taylor: (2) No, I ________. In fact, (3) ________ (I / never / be) in an action movie before.
Reporter: Wow! What about Dario? (4) ________ (you / ever / work) with him?
Rob Taylor: (5) Yes, I ________. (6) ________ (we / make) three movies together. But this movie was the best. (7) ________ (I / never / have) such a good time.

___ /14

Present perfect with *already*, *yet*, and *just*

4 Write the complete conversation using the present perfect and simple past.

Ana: Do you want to see the new Rob Taylor movie?
Bob: (1) I / already / see / it.
____
Ana: (2) When / you / see / it?
____
Bob: (3) I / go / last week / with Marc.
____
Ana: (4) you / enjoy / it?
____
Bob: (5) Yes. They / just / start / filming Part 2.
____
Ana: (6) you / see / *Final Destination* / yet?
____
Bob: (7) No, I / not see / it / yet.
____

___ /14

Your score: ___ /50

SKILLS CHECK

✓✓✓ Yes, I can. No problem!
✓✓ Yes, I can. But I need a little help.
✓ Yes, I can. But I need a lot of help.

I can identify the author's argument when I read. ________
I can use the audio type to help me understand. ________
I can talk about problems. ________
I can agree and disagree with someone. ________
I can give my opinion when I write. ________

Workbook, pages 110–111

READ

1 Look at each text. What does it say? Choose the correct summary (A, B, or C).

TEST-TAKING TIPS

match short texts to summaries

- Look at each text. What kind of text is it?
- Read the text. What is its general meaning?
- Read the three summaries carefully.
- Look for specific information in the text to help choose your answer.

1

PART-TIME DRIVER
needed for local company. You don't have to be experienced, but you must be 16 or over.

What are the conditions of the job offer?
A You must have experience.
B You need a degree.
C You have to be older than 15.

2

Did you see a crime here last Monday?
The victim was a local artist. Please help Springfield police identify and arrest the thief.

A The police need help to find a criminal.
B The police are looking for a local artist.
C The police know the identity of the criminal.

3

Hi, Jan. I've gone to the hair salon.
Back soon. Lunch is in the refrigerator.
I've already given some food to the cats.
Ally.

What should Jan do?
A Give food to the cats.
B Have something to eat.
C Meet Ally at the hair salon.

4

PRIORITY SEATING
These seats are for the elderly, people with disabilities, and people carrying children.

A You mustn't put your feet on the seats.
B Give the seats to other people if they need them more than you.
C You have to pay extra to use these seats.

5

Sarah is turning 16! Please come to a surprise party on **Saturday** at **9 p.m.**
There'll be lots of food and games!
Don't be late or it won't be a surprise!!

If you go to the party,
A you must bring some food.
B you have to be 16 or older.
C you mustn't arrive after nine o'clock.

Reading: ______ /10

LISTEN

2 (▶43) **Look at the five sentences. You'll hear a conversation between two friends, Beth and Matt, about a TV series and a movie. Check (✓) T if each sentence is true or F if it's false.**

		T	F
1	*Tara Stone* is the title of a science fiction television series.	☐	☐
2	In each episode, Tara travels into the future to find some criminals.	☐	☐
3	Beth wants Matt to watch the series.	☐	☐
4	Beth hasn't watched all of the documentary yet.	☐	☐
5	Matt agrees with Beth's opinion of the documentary.	☐	☐

Listening: ______ /10

WRITE

3 Read part of an email message from your American penpal Dani. Then write an email message (80–100 words) and answer Dani's questions.

> What kinds of TV shows do you like? Why do you like them? I love comedy shows. Have you ever watched any American TV shows? Do you ever watch TV shows in English? Write and tell me.

Writing: ______ /10

Progress check score ______ /30

TEST-TAKING TIPS

answer true/false questions

- Read the sentences carefully before you listen.
- Every part of the sentence must be true; listen carefully for the details.
- When you listen again, check your answers.
- If you don't know, guess – you have a 50 percent chance of being right.

TEST-TAKING TIPS

reply to an email message

- Read the task. Who are you writing to?
- Read the email and underline the points to include.
- Plan your email before you write.
- Include phrases to start and end your message.

UNIT 9 SPORTS REPORT

IN THE PICTURE Strange sports

>>> Talk about sports and sports equipment

WORK WITH WORDS

1 RECALL **Work in pairs. Write lists of sports under the headings. You have three minutes.**

Ball sports	Water sports	Winter sports	Other
basketball	*sailing*	*ice hockey*	*dancing*

2 **Look at the big photos. Describe the two sports.**

PHRASE BYTES

It looks like … but … It's a mixture of … and …

3 ▶44 **Look at the equipment in the small photos. Listen and repeat.**

4 **Work in pairs. Take the quiz. Then write two more questions for another pair.**

5 a **What equipment can you see in the big photos?**

In the first photo I can see a snorkel and …

b ▶45 **Listen to information about the sports in the photos. Complete the notes under the headings.**

QUIZ: Do you know your sports?

For what sport (or sports) do you need …

1. a ball, a net, and a racket?
2. a ball and a stick?
3. a board, warm clothes, and a helmet?
4. a ball, special shoes, and two goals?
5. a bat and a ball?
6. a ball and two hoops?
7. skates?
8. a mask, snorkel, and flippers?

	OCTOPUSH	SEPAK TAKRAW
POPULAR IN:	Australia, New Zealand, (1) *South Africa*, ______, ______	Southeast (7) ______
NUMBER OF PLAYERS:	(2) ______	(8) ______
EQUIPMENT:	2 goals, (3) ______	volleyball net, (9) ______
CLOTHES:	swimsuit/trunks, (4) ______, ______	shorts, (10) ______, ______
GOAL OF THE GAME:	to get (5) ______	to get (11) ______
WHY PLAY?	fast and (6) ______	exciting and (12) ______

OCTOPUSH

SEPAK TAKRAW

6 **THE MOVING PICTURE** **Watch the video of two other sports. Would you like to play these games? Why or why not?**

SPEAK

7 **Write facts about a popular sport or your favorite sport. Use Exercise 5b to help you. Tell your partner about your sport.**

MOVE BEYOND

Do the Words & Beyond exercise on page 68.

Workbook, page 112

READING Soccer and fair play

»» Understand pronouns

SPEAK AND READ

1 Work in pairs. Answer the questions.

1 Do you play soccer? Do you watch soccer? Why or why not?
2 Why do you think soccer is so popular?
3 What do you think people can learn from soccer?

2 Students at Pinewood Middle School have done a project. Look at the photos and headings. What do you think the project is about? Decide if the sentences are correct (*C*) or incorrect (*I*).

1 Soccer is a sport for everybody. *C*
2 You can't play soccer without the right equipment. ____
3 You can learn important life skills from soccer. ____
4 Soccer causes strong feelings. ____
5 Street soccer is like normal soccer but in the street. ____
6 In street soccer, a girl has to score the first goal. ____

3 ▶46 Read the report to check your answers to Exercise 2.

Pinewood
MIDDLE SCHOOL

Our sports report: Soccer and fair play

Soccer is a sport that brings people together. Millions of people play soccer and billions of people watch it. You don't need expensive equipment for soccer. You can play it in the street without a soccer field, proper goals, expensive soccer shoes, or a real ball. And soccer, like many other sports, teaches you skills that are useful in all areas of life: teamwork and respect for others.

Unfortunately, the love that people have for soccer can also cause conflict. Players sometimes disagree about the rules, so every soccer game has a referee. The referee can give the other team a free kick or penalty if a player breaks the rules, or he can send the player off the field. Sometimes players and fans get angry if they don't like the referee's decision and their team loses. They can become violent.

A German university teacher who was living in Colombia was worried about the violence in soccer. He decided to do something about it. He started a street soccer project for young people in Medellín which was called Fútbol por la Paz (Soccer for Peace). It has different rules than normal soccer. Fair play is more important than goals. Street soccer was very successful in Medellín, and it became popular in many Latin American countries. Today people play it all over the world.

The rules of street soccer

There are two teams and four players on a team.
There are no goalkeepers.
Each team must include boys and girls.
A girl must score at least one goal – or the other goals don't count.
The team that wins gets three points, and the team that loses gets one point.
Each team gets two points for a tie (e.g., 1–1, 2–2).
If they play fair, teams can get extra points.

4 a Read the tips in the HOW TO box.

b Read the report again. Circle the pronoun *it* in paragraphs 1 and 3. Which nouns does the pronoun *it* replace?

5 Which tips in the HOW TO box did you use for help with Exercise 4b? Check (✓) them.

HOW TO
understand pronouns

☐ Find the pronoun (e.g, *I / me, you / you, he / him, she / her, it / it, we / us, they / them*).
☐ Identify the correct noun (e.g., *sport, players*) for the pronoun. A pronoun usually comes AFTER the noun.
☐ Replace the pronoun with a noun. If it sounds wrong, find another noun.

REACT

6 Work in pairs. Which sentences do you agree with? Why?

1 I think soccer is a great way for kids to learn skills.
2 I think soccer can help people live in peace.
3 I'd like to try street soccer.

MOVE BEYOND

Circle all the soccer and equipment words in the text.

Workbook, page 113

GRAMMAR Relative clauses

>>> Use relative clauses to describe people, things, and places

READ >>> Grammar in context

1 Read about a mystery sport. Which sport is it?

Mystery sport facts

People **who** don't like soccer often enjoy sports **that** are less physical. This is an example of a relaxing sport **which** has a very long history. The ancient Egyptians were the first people **who** played it – 5,000 years ago! Today it's the game **that** people in the USA most like to play. It's also very popular in Japan **where** you can find the world's biggest alley – it has 156 lanes!

STUDY

2 Look at the relative pronouns in bold in Exercise 1. Circle the noun before each pronoun. Then complete the explanations with *that*, *which*, *who*, or *where*.

Relative clauses

Use relative clauses to identify or describe people, things, and places.

Use ________ and ________ for people.
Use ________ and ________ for things.
Use ________ for places.

See GRAMMAR DATABASE, page 63.

PRACTICE

3 a Read the facts and choose the correct relative pronoun. If both pronouns are possible, choose both.

Skiing facts

1. Skiing is a method of transportation *who* / *which* Asians and North Europeans have used for thousands of years.
2. "Ski" is an old Norwegian word *which* / *that* means "stick of wood."
3. Modern skis are plastic, but there are places in China *that* / *where* people still make skis from wood and horse skin.
4. It was Sherlock Holmes creator Arthur Conan-Doyle *which* / *who* made skiing a popular vacation activity in the Swiss Alps.
5. Extreme skiing is a sport *that* / *where* started in Switzerland in the mid-1960s.
6. The first person *who* / *that* skied down Mount Everest was extreme skier Slovenian Davo Karnicar in 2000.

b Which fact do you think is the most interesting? Why?

4 a Complete the sports facts with the correct pronoun(s).

Sports facts

1. The two tallest men *who/that* played basketball for the National Basketball Association were ____ meters tall.
2. The longest tennis match was a game ________ lasted ____ hours and five minutes.
3. In ancient Greece, the people ________ ran in races put ____ on their skin.
4. It was an engineer from Britain ________ invented ____. He wanted a sport ________ he could play indoors when it rained.
5. The strangest place ________ people have played golf is on the ____.
6. The score ________ is most common in a soccer World Cup final is ____.

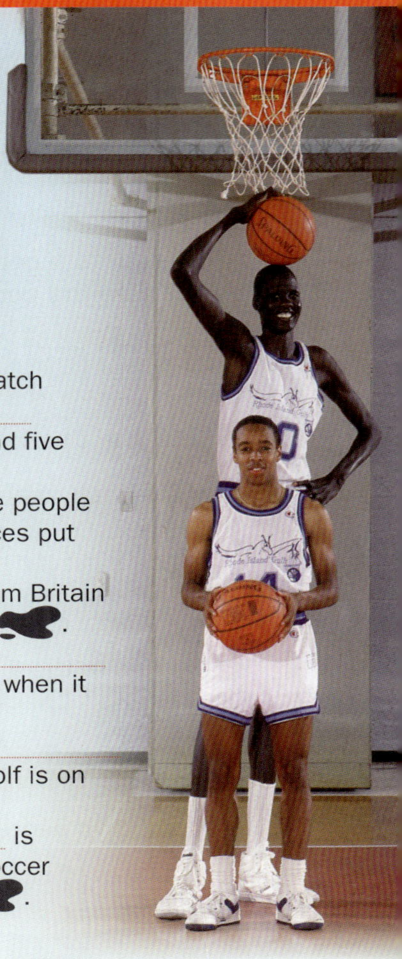

b Work in pairs. Decide which words or numbers are behind the ____. Then check your answers on page 141.

WRITE AND SPEAK

5 a Complete the sentences about you.

1. The sports that I play are …
2. The place where I most often play sports is …
3. The sports that I watch on TV are …
4. The sport that I like best is …
5. The sports hero who I like the most is …

b Guess your partner's answers.

The sports that you play are soccer and swimming.

Yes, that's right. / No, the sports that I play are …

Workbook, pages 114–115

LISTENING AND VOCABULARY Sports fans

Listen for specific information

SPEAK AND LISTEN

1 Work in pairs. Look at the photo of the baseball fans. Say …

1 what they are wearing.
2 why they look like this.
3 how you think they feel.

2 47 Listen to a conversation with Liam, another baseball fan. Choose the correct options.

1 Liam is a *Red Sox* / *Yankees* fan.
2 Liam is going to a baseball game with *his dad* / *a reporter*.
3 The *Red Sox* / *Yankees* win the game.

3 a Read the tips in the HOW TO box.

b 47 Listen again and complete the sentences.

1 Before the game Liam feels really relaxed .
2 At the baseball field Liam feels really ______ .
3 During the game Liam thinks the Sox will ______ .
4 The final score is ______ .

4 Which tips in the HOW TO box did you use for help with Exercise 3b? Check (✓) them.

HOW TO
listen for specific information

- ☐ Look at the task. Decide what you want to know.
- ☐ Think about the topic and words you might hear. Use words in the task to help you.
- ☐ Take notes as you listen if it helps you.

WORK WITH WORDS

5 Read the two quotes below from the listening text. Then answer the questions.

a "And how do you feel right now? Are you **relaxed** or **worried**?"
b "It's **amazing**. Games between the Sox and the Yankees are always more **exciting** than other games."

1 Which adjectives describe a feeling? What ending do they have?
2 Which adjectives describe what you think of something? What ending do they have?

6 48 Complete the pairs of words. Then listen and check.

1 I felt relax*ed* . It was very relax*ing* .
2 It was an amaz___ experience! I'm amaz___ at how good the team was.
3 I was so excit___ about the tennis match. It was really excit___ to watch it in person.
4 I was interest___ in watching him. He's an interest___ player.
5 It was a really depress___ game! I feel so depress___ .
6 I was disappoint___ by the result. It was very disappoint___ .
7 I was really annoy___ at the referee. His decisions were very annoy___ .
8 The players were embarrass___ . I was embarrass___ for the team.
9 I was so bor___ . It was a very bor___ game.
10 Today's score is worry___ . I'm worri___ about the next game.

7 49 PRONOUNCE Listen to the adjectives in Exercise 6. Underline the stressed syllable in each adjective. Then listen again and repeat the adjectives.

REACT

8 Work in pairs. Ask and answer the questions to the right.

Are you a sports fan?

Yes

1 *Do you feel relaxed or excited when you watch sports? Why?*
2 *Which team or sports person do you think is the most amazing?*
3 *How do you feel when your team or favorite player loses?*

No

1 *What sports do you find the most boring?*
2 *How do other people in your family feel about sports?*
3 *What activities do you find exciting or interesting?*

MOVE BEYOND

Do the Words & Beyond exercise on page 68.

Workbook, pages 116–117

GRAMMAR Comparisons

»» Compare people, things, and places

READ »» Grammar in context

1 **Read about John. What does John collect? How does he help others?**

The greatest and **most exciting** feeling for a sports card fan is opening a pack of cards. John Makowiec was collecting sports cards before he was **old enough** to go to school. Ten years later, he started "Cards2Kids." He wanted to give sports cards to kids who **weren't as lucky as** he was – kids in the hospital with serious or **less serious** illnesses, or kids from **the least wealthy** families in the area.

John asked people for cards, and they were **more generous** than he expected! He was **too busy** to pack all the cards himself. Luckily some of his friends were **as excited as** he was about the idea and decided to help him.

STUDY

2 **Complete the explanations with the items in the box.**

-er -ier more -est -iest most

Comparative and superlative adjectives

Use comparative adjectives to compare two things.
For one-syllable adjectives, add __________ + *than*.
For two-syllable adjectives that end in *-y*, add __________ + *than*.
For two or more syllables, use __________ + adj + *than*.

Use superlative adjectives to compare more than two things.
For one-syllable adjectives, add *the* + __________.
For two-syllable adjectives that end in *-y*, add *the* __________.
For two or more syllables, use *the* __________.

Less is the opposite of *more*. *The least* is the opposite of *the most*.

See GRAMMAR DATABASE, page 63.

3 **Underline expressions with *as*, *too*, and *enough* in Exercise 1.**

Equality and inequality

Use *as … as* to compare things that are the same.

Use *not as … as* to compare things that are different.

Use *too* + adjective to indicate a problem.

Use *enough* to say you have as much as you need.

Use *not enough* to say you need more of something.

See GRAMMAR DATABASE, page 63.

PRACTICE

4 **Julia and Yan are basketball fans and collect sports cards. They're comparing three basketball players. Complete their conversation.**

Julia: Ty's the (1) *best* (**good**) player!
Yan: He's (2) __________ (**tall**) than the others, but he isn't (3) __________ (**good**) than they are. I think Florian's a (4) __________ (**exciting**) player than Ty.
Julia: Well, he's the (5) __________ (**smart**) player. But I still think Ty's the (6) __________ (**exciting**). I don't like Kosuke. Kosuke's the (7) __________ (**interesting**).
Yan: Yes, I agree, he's definitely (8) __________ (**interesting**) than the other two.

5 **a** **Yan's also a fan of a different sport. Complete Yan's sentences so that they have the same meaning. Use no more than three words.**

1. Baseball is too boring for me.
   Baseball isn't *exciting enough* for me.
2. In my favorite sport, the paddle is smaller than a baseball bat.
   The paddle isn't as __________ a baseball bat.
3. The ball is lighter than a baseball.
   The ball isn't as __________ a baseball.
4. It's popular in the USA but also popular in Asia.
   It's as popular __________ in the USA.
5. It's easy enough for small children to play.
   It isn't too __________ for small children to play.
6. A lot of people are too slow to play this sport well.
   A lot of people aren't __________ to play this sport well.

b **Which sport is Yan describing?**

WRITE AND SPEAK

6 **a** **With the class, make a list of popular sports stars on the board.**

b **Work in pairs. Compare the stars using words from the box.**

active bad smart dangerous exciting fast in shape lazy slow tall young

PHRASE BYTES

I think … is the best / is the least …

… is faster than … / not as smart as … / too …

That's true. / I don't agree. I think …

»» Workbook, page 118

LANGUAGE & BEYOND

Yesterday I fell down when we were playing baseball, and I dropped the ball. All the other boys made silly comments, and I was so embarassed. Last night I couldn't sleep, and I have a headache. I feel really angry – why were they so mean?

EMMA

I get really worried, and sometimes I feel like I can't breathe. I have so many things to do – I have a lot of homework, but I also have piano lessons and concerts. I'm on the basketball team, and I have gymnastics practice every week too.

JOE

TOM

I can't concentrate on my homework now, and I have a stomachache. I have to give a speech this week, and I hate talking in front of the class. I always get really nervous. Then I forget things and feel dumb.

Learn to deal with stress

KNOW YOURSELF

READ

1 a Look at the photos. Why might the students be stressed?

b Read the students' speech bubbles. Match them to the reasons.

1 an embarrassing moment 2 busy days 3 school work

2 Write lists of the way the students show stress.

Body	Mind	Feelings
can't breathe		

3 Work in pairs. Talk about the situations. Can you understand how they feel? Have you ever felt like this?

DO

4 Look at the tips to beat stress. Work in pairs. Answer the questions.

1 Which tips are especially important for Emma, Joe, or Tom?
2 Which tips can help all the students?

REFLECT

5 Discuss the questions with your class. Do you agree with the REFLECTION POINT?

1 Do you think the tips in Exercise 4 can help? Why or why not?
2 Do you have other tips for stressed students?

EXTEND

6 Work in pairs. Look at the posters on page 72, then make your own "Keep calm" poster.

EIGHT great stress beaters!

1 Try and forget problems and do something that you enjoy: meet friends or listen to music.
2 Do sports regularly. You'll feel more relaxed.
3 Organize your time.
4 Talk to your parents, a teacher, or another adult.
5 Think positively: make a list of good things in your life.
6 Take five deep breaths. Breathe in through your nose and out through your mouth.
7 Sleep for at least eight hours a night. (When you're very tired, you feel more stressed.)
8 Make a plan to prepare for a stressful situation in the future.

REFLECTION POINT

Take care of your body and mind: sleep well, play sports, and do things that make you happy.

Try to change the situations that make you stressed (if you can).

Workbook, page 121

SPEAKING Winners and losers

Congratulate and sympathize with people

SPEAK

1 **Work in pairs. Look at the photos. How do you think the people feel?**

I think the girls in photo a feel amazed and very happy.

LISTEN

2 **50 Read and listen to the conversations (1–5). Match them to the correct photos in Exercise 1 (a–e).**

1 **Inez:** No, that's not fair! It should be our ball.
Claudia: **Too bad!** That was close … Don't get mad or you'll get a yellow card. *d*

2 **Nick:** This is just the best day ever!
Finn: **You did a great job!** I hate to say it, but you were better than I was today. ____

3 **Kathy:** Oh, no, I really wanted to win this one … **congratulations**!
Cindy: Thanks. **Better luck next time**! ____

4 **Kurt:** Oh, no, that was terrible …
Rachel: **Never mind**. Everybody has bad days … **I know how you feel**, but it's not that bad. ____

5 **Becky:** I don't believe it! We did it! We won!
Ellen: **Good job!** Wow, that was just – **you were amazing!** ____

3 **50 Listen to the conversations and check your answers.**

4 **50 Listen again and look at the phrases in bold. Which phrases do you use when …**

1 you congratulate another person (tell the person he or she has done well)?
2 you sympathize with another person (are nice when the person has lost or not done very well)?

ACT

5 **a** **Work in pairs.**

Student A: Read one of your lines in the box out loud.
Student B: Congratulate or sympathize.

Student A
1 Yes! That was the best game that I've ever played!
2 I can't believe it. I won!
3 Oh, no, that was terrible …

b **Student B: Read one of your lines in the box out loud.**
Student A: Congratulate or sympathize.

Student B
1 Last place again. How embarrassing …
2 I did it! I did it! I really did it!
3 That was the worst game that I've ever played.

6 **Work in pairs. Write your own conversation and then present it to another pair.**

a

b

c

d

e

PHRASEBOOK 51

Congratulate somebody
Congratulations!
Good job!
You were amazing / fantastic.
You did a great job.

Sympathize with somebody
Too bad!
Better luck next time!
Never mind.
I know how you feel.

Workbook, page 119

WRITING My sports report

Use pronouns

SPEAK AND READ

1 Work in pairs. Answer the questions.

1 Do you like running? Why or why not?
2 Have you ever done a race (or a walk) to collect money for charity (e.g., a hospital)? Who was it for?
3 Have you ever watched a marathon in your town or on TV? What was it like?

2 Look at the photos and read about the New York Marathon. Where was the winner from? How fast was his time?

The New York Marathon is one of the biggest marathons in the world. This year, the number of runners who finished the marathon was 46,795. Some of the people who ran to collect money for charity were in funny costumes. I saw a lot of superheroes like Superwoman and Captain America, but the strangest costume that I saw was a yellow man. The costume that I liked the best was a sumo wrestler.

The winner of the marathon was from Kenya. He won the marathon in two hours, five minutes, and six seconds. His time was the fastest time ever! The most exciting moment was in the women's race when a runner from Ethiopia passed the favorite in the last mile and won.

3 a Read the tips in the HOW TO box.

HOW TO
use relative pronouns to combine sentences

- Use the correct pronoun for the noun.
- Change *a / an* to *the*.
- Don't use another pronoun with a relative pronoun.
  I saw a marathon. The marathon was very exciting.
  *The marathon **that I saw** ~~it~~ was very exciting.*

b In the report, underline four relative pronouns and the clause after them. What nouns do the relative clauses describe? Circle them.

PRACTICE

4 Make these sentences sound more natural. Combine the sentences with relative pronouns.

1 A group of people do the marathon in wheelchairs. They're very fast.
2 The people in wheelchairs follow a route. It's the same route as the runners' route.
3 A man won the marathon wheelchair race this year. He was from Japan.

DISCUSS

5 Discuss an international, local, or school sports event.

WRITE

6 Write a sportscast about the event you discussed.

1 Describe the sports event. Explain where the game, match, or race was. Tell who the teams, players, or athletes were.
2 Give interesting information about the players using relative clauses. Describe the players or the sport with *who, which,* or *that. The team that won yesterday will go to the finals.* See the HOW TO box.
3 Describe what happened and the result. Use comparatives and superlatives. Describe the most exciting moment, the better team, the best athlete, or the highest score.

SHARE

7 Present your sportscast to a small group or your class. Which is the most interesting sport? Which was the most exciting event?

Workbook, pages 120–121

VOCABULARY Sports equipment

1 Write the correct word for the description.

The All Stars ★★★★★ Sports Academy

Know your equipment!

1 p ______ : you hit a table tennis ball with it
2 r ______ : you hit a tennis ball with it
3 s ______ : you hold it when you play hockey
4 p ______ : you hit it when you play hockey
5 b ______ : you hit a ball with it in baseball
6 f ______ : you wear them on your feet for swimming
7 s ______ : you breathe with it underwater
8 h ______ : you wear it on your head to protect it
9 s ______ : you wear them on your feet and go fast
10 h ______ : you put a basketball in it
11 g ______ : you kick or throw balls into it
12 n ______ : you hit a ball over it

___ /12

-ed and *-ing* adjectives

2 Read the comments by students at the sports academy. Choose the correct options.

1 The mountain bike race was *amazed* / *amazing*.
2 I'm so *excited* / *exciting* about going sailing.
3 I'm really *interested* / *interesting* in surfing.
4 The horseback riding course is very *relaxed* / *relaxing*.
5 I was so bad at hockey, it was *depressed* / *depressing*.
6 I'm *disappointed* / *disappointing* that there's no kayaking.
7 It's so *annoyed* / *annoying* that we lost the volleyball game.
8 I was a little *bored* / *boring* in the tennis class.
9 The dance class was really *embarrassed* / *embarrassing*!
10 I'm *worried* / *worrying* about the swimming test.

___ /10

GRAMMAR Relative clauses

3 Complete the descriptions with the correct relative pronouns. If you can use two pronouns, write them both.

The All Stars ★★★★★ Sports Academy

Know your sports and where you play them!

1 Baseball is a game ______ Americans play.
2 Snowboarding is a sport for people ______ love danger.
3 A court is ______ you play tennis or basketball.
4 Basketball is a sport for players ______ are tall.
5 Skiing is a sport ______ you do in winter.
6 A field is ______ you play football, soccer, or rugby.

___ /12

Comparisons

4 Complete what the trainers said about the students. Use the correct form of the adjectives.

1 Barbara was almost ______ (**amazing**) as I was on the tennis court!
2 Rose was ______ (**small**) than the other basketball players – but still fantastic!
3 Matt was ______ (**relaxed**) than all the other surfers!
4 Flora was just too ______ (**smart**) for all the other volleyball players!
5 Eva was the ______ (**exciting**) table tennis player this year!
6 Finn wasn't ______ (**quick**) as the other cyclists but he was still great!
7 Theo was the ______ (**fast**) runner this year!
8 Rafael wasn't ______ (**good**) enough to be on the team, but he tried very hard!

___ /16

Your score: ___ /50

SKILLS CHECK

✓✓✓ Yes, I can. No problem!
✓✓ Yes, I can. But I need a little help.
✓ Yes, I can. But I need a lot of help.

I can understand pronouns when I read. ______
I can listen for specific information. ______
I can deal with stress. ______
I can congratulate and sympathize with people. ______
I can use pronouns when I write. ______

Workbook, pages 122–123

find

FIND IT!

UNIT 10 BRAINWAVES

IN THE PICTURE Science Museum

>>> Talk about inventions and materials

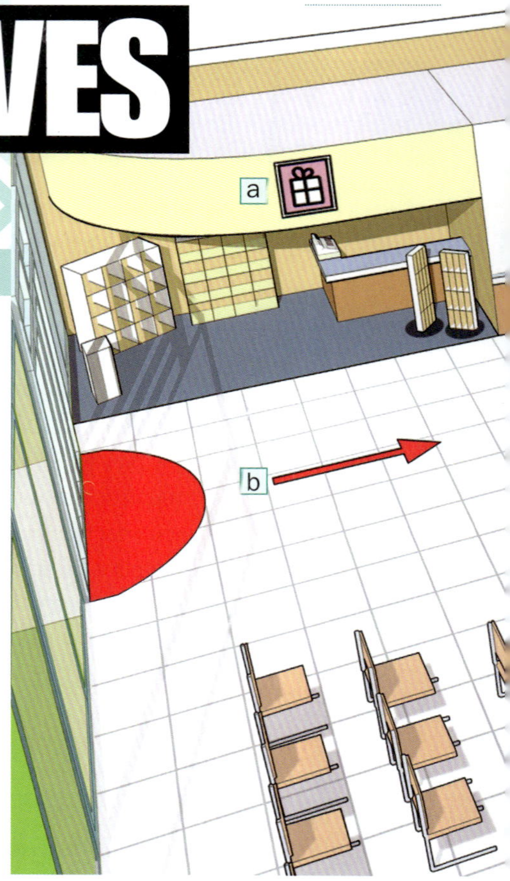

WORK WITH WORDS

1 RECALL **Work in pairs. Match the words in the box to the pictures (a–j). You have one minute.**

___ coffee shop	___ elevator	___ entrance	___ second floor
___ gift shop	___ first floor	___ information desk	
___ restrooms	___ stairs	___ ticket office	

2 **Work in pairs. Match the words to galleries G1–G4 in the museum and complete the mind maps.**

~~build~~ calculate create design develop discover explore glass plastic produce metal stone

3 52 **Listen and check or complete your answers. Then listen and repeat.**

4 THE MOVING PICTURE **Watch the museum presentation. Can you remember the pictures for the words in Exercise 2? Work in pairs and make a list.**

5 **Match materials from Exercise 2 to the things in the museum. You can match more than one material to each object.**

chair desk elevator entrance doors floor stairs

Chair – wood, ...

6 **Choose the best word (A, B, or C) for each space in the ad to the right.**

	A	B	C
1	built	developed	calculated
2	create	build	explore
3	built	explored	found
4	create	produce	discover
5	calculate	develop	design
6	explored	discovered	designed
7	calculate	create	invent
8	designed	produced	found

7 53 PRONOUNCE **Listen to the sentences. Underline the /v/ sound. Then listen again and repeat the sentences.**

Hoover invented the vacuum cleaner.
Every discovery's a brainwave.
Very smart brains develop mobile devices.

We are SCIENCE!

We have (1) ________ the technology to send people into space and (2) ________ the moon. We have (3) ________ telescopes that can see far into the universe. We have used them to (4) ________ new planets, and to (5) ________ the size and age of stars. Back on Earth, we have (6) ________ machines that see inside our bodies and (7) ________ 3D images of our brain. And we have (8) ________ medicine that helps us live longer, healthier lives.

COME AND SEE US AT THE SCIENCE MUSEUM!

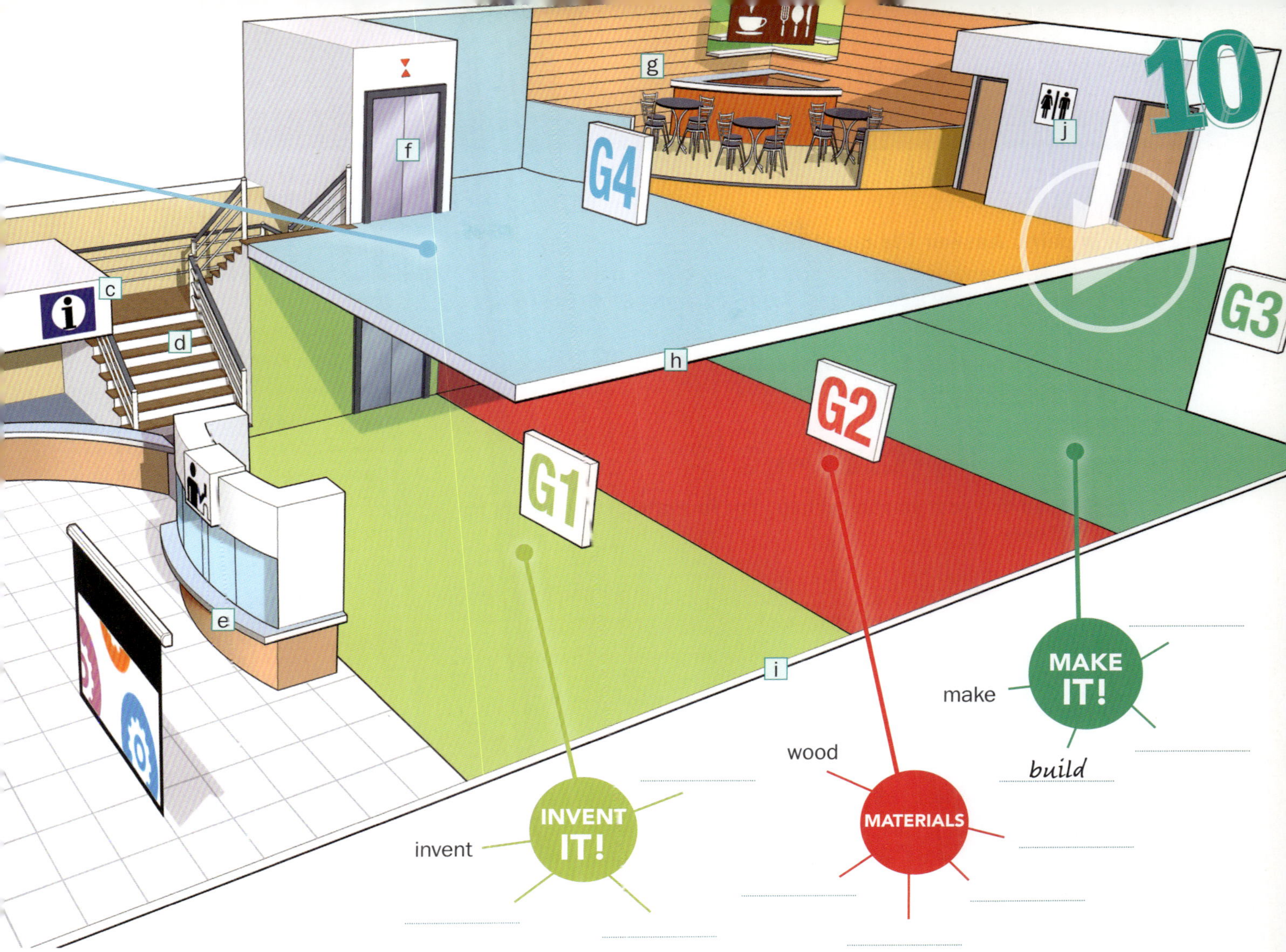

8 **Take the science quiz. Then check your answers on page 71.**

Test your knowledge of science with our science quiz. Click to choose your answer.

1 He invented the phonograph, the first machine that could record sound. Who was he?

A Henry Ford | B Thomas Edison | C Guglielmo Marconi

2 In which year did humans first explore the moon?

A 1956 | B 1969 | C 1982

3 Gustave Eiffel's company designed and built the Eiffel Tower in 1889. How tall is it?

A 820 meters | B 520 meters | C 320 meters

4 It came before the invention of metal objects. What was it called?

A The Stone Age | B The Iron Age | C The Wood Age

PHRASE BYTES

There isn't a science museum here, but there's one in …

Yes, I have. I've been to the science museum in …

No, I haven't, but I'd like to go to one because …

SPEAK

9 **Work in pairs. Answer the questions.**

1 Is there a science museum in your town or city? Where is it? If not, where's the nearest one?

2 Have you ever been to a science museum?
If so, what did you see? Did you enjoy your visit? Why or why not?
If not, would you like to go to one? Why or why not?

MOVE BEYOND

Do the Words & Beyond exercise on page 69.

Workbook, page 124

READING How it works

Use pictures for help with new words

SPEAK AND READ

1 Work in pairs. Answer the questions.

1 Do you like science subjects at school? Why or why not?
2 Can you explain how a cell phone, TV, or radio works – in English or in your own language?

2 Read the first paragraph below and complete the sentences.

1 The British English for *cell phone* is …
2 Today's cell phones can …

3 a Read the tips in the HOW TO box.

b 54 Read the rest of the article. Try to match new words to the pictures.

HOW TO
use pictures for help with new words

- ☐ Look at the pictures. What do they show? What's the text about?
- ☐ Read the text. When you see a new word, look at the pictures. Can you see the word in the pictures?

In the UK they're called mobile phones, mobiles, or just phones. In the USA they're called cell phones. From the days of calling and texting at the start of this century, they've developed into small computers that can do anything a PC or laptop can do.

But how do they work?

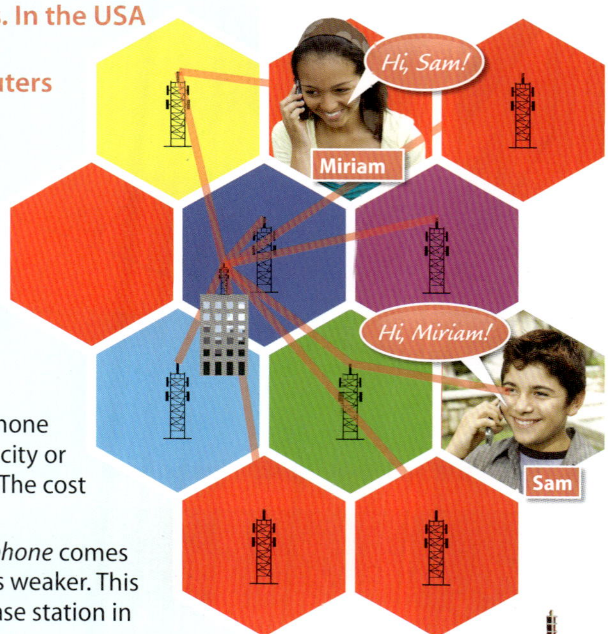

To understand cell phone technology, the first thing you need to know is that a cell phone is really a two-way radio. When Miriam calls Sam, her voice is changed into a digital radio signal.

This radio signal is sent by her phone to the closest base station on her phone company's network. A base station has radio equipment inside and an antenna on top. In cities you can see base stations on the roofs of many buildings.

From the base station her call is connected to her company's Mobile Telephone Switching Office (MTSO). All the calls from the base stations in a particular city or area are sent here. The MTSO connects her call to a base station near Sam. The cost of the call is also calculated here.

Each base station is in the middle of an area called a cell. (The "cell" in *cell phone* comes from here.) If you move into another cell during a call, your signal becomes weaker. This change is seen by computers at the MTSO, and your call is passed to the base station in the new cell. This happens very quickly, and you don't notice the change.

It's these cells that make it possible for us all to have cell phones. Each phone company can only use a limited number of frequencies for its calls. With cells, people can use the same frequencies in different parts of a city. And that means more people can use their phones at the same time.

4 Which tips in the HOW TO box did you use for help with Exercise 3b? Check (✓) them.

5 Read the article again and write your answers to the questions.

1 What does a cell phone do to your voice when you speak?
It changes it into a digital radio signal.
2 In cities, where do companies put a lot of their base stations?
3 Where do all the phone calls in a city go?
4 Why are mobile phones called cell phones in the USA?
5 How does the cell phone network know if you're moving?
6 Why are cells so important to cell phone companies?

REACT

6 Work in pairs. What do you think? Tell your partner.

1 Was the explanation of how a cell phone works easy or hard to understand? Why?
2 Do you think it's interesting to understand how things work? Why or why not?

PHRASE BYTES

I think it was easy / hard to understand because …

I think it's really interesting / boring because …

MOVE BEYOND

Work in pairs. Practice explaining how a cell phone works. Can you do it without looking at the article?

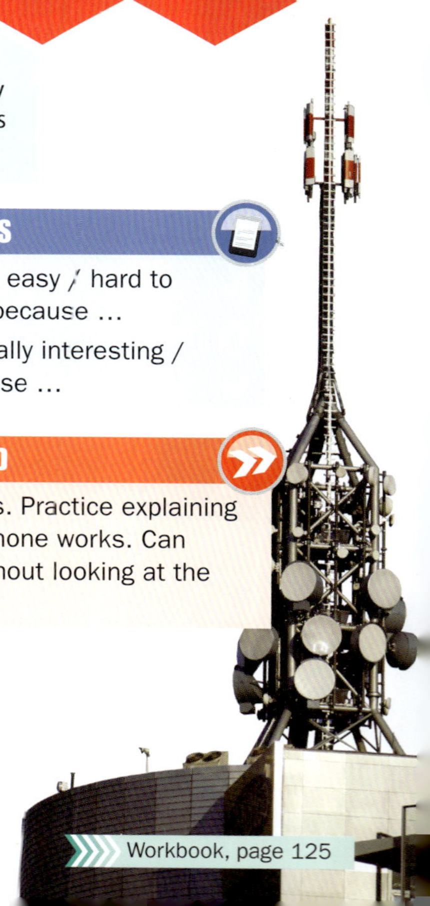

Workbook, page 125

GRAMMAR Simple present passive

>>> Use the simple present passive to talk about facts and processes

READ >>> Grammar in context

1 **Read the article and find two reasons why you should recycle cell phones.**

RECYCLE YOUR CELL PHONE!

Most people use a cell phone. But what **is** a cell phone **made** of? We all know that a cell phone **is** mainly **made** of plastic and metal, but did you know that dangerous chemicals **are** also **used**? This is one good reason for recycling them. Small amounts of rare, expensive metals **are needed** too. These metals **are thrown away** and lost if a cell phone **isn't recycled**. So when you need a new cell phone, recycle your old one!

STUDY

2 **The verbs in green in Exercise 1 are in the simple present passive. Use them to complete the explanations.**

Simple present passive

Use the passive when the action is more important than the person who does the action.

Most people use cell phones. (active voice)

Cell phones are made of metal and plastic. (passive voice)

Affirmative and negative

To form the passive in the simple present tense, use *am, is, are* + (*not*) + past participle.

These metals .... thrown away and lost if a cell phone .... recycled.

Questions

To form a question in the simple present passive, use this word order:

am, is, are + subject + past participle

What .... a cell phone .... of?

See GRAMMAR DATABASE, page 64.

PRACTICE

3 **Complete the description with the past participle form of the verbs.**

How are cell phones made?

First, a number of designs are (1) presented (**present**). One design is (2) .... (**choose**) and engineers then decide what electronics and software are (3) .... (**need**). Next, the phone is (4) .... (**make**), but it isn't (5) .... (**send**) to stores yet. First, it is (6) .... (**test**) to be sure there are no problems. Then it's ready to sell.

4 **a** **Complete the sentences with the simple present passive form of the verbs.**

1. Ninety percent of the world's products are transported (**transport**) this way.
2. Most cell phones .... (**not / protect**) against them.
3. The meat of this animal .... (**not / eat**) in India.
4. These games .... (**play**) on a board with 64 squares.
5. This food .... (**grow**) in very wet fields.
6. This language .... (**speak**) by more than a billion people.

b **What things do the sentences describe?**

5 **a** **Write questions in the simple present passive.**

1. Where / most cell phones / make / ?
   Where are most cell phones made?
2. Why / texting / use / more than calling on cell phones?
   ....
3. What ingredients / pasta / make / of?
   ....
4. When / Earth Day / celebrate?
   ....
5. What sports / play / on a court?
   ....
6. Where / Portuguese / speak / as a native language?
   ....

b **Work in pairs. Answer the questions.**

WRITE AND SPEAK

6 **Work in pairs. Write definitions of three different things. Then read your definitions to other students. Can they identify the things?**

They're made of plastic, metal, and glass. They're used to talk to a person in another place.

Cell phones!

>>> Workbook, pages 126–127

LISTENING AND VOCABULARY Everyday objects

Understand new words

SPEAK AND LISTEN

1 Work in pairs. Look at the photos and answer the questions.

1 How many of the objects can you name in English?
2 What are the objects used for?

2 a Read the tips in the HOW TO box.

b 55 Listen to an excerpt from a museum audio guide. Write the letter of each object the guide describes.

Object 1 ...... Object 3 ...... Object 5 ......
Object 2 ...... Object 4 ......

3 Which tips in the HOW TO box did you use for help with Exercise 2b? Check (✓) them.

WORK WITH WORDS

4 56 Listen and point to the correct everyday object in the photos. Then listen and repeat.

ballpoint pen clothespin thumbtack light bulb can

5 55 Listen to the museum audio guide again and complete the sentences with the words in Exercise 4.

1 The *thumbtack* is called a drawing pin in British English.
2 The original .... was made of wood.
3 The .... was produced by the American inventor Thomas Alva Edison.
4 The .... was invented by two Hungarian brothers.
5 The .... was invented by a Paris chef.

6 57 Match everyday objects to the photos. Then match the definitions to the words. Listen and repeat.

bottle caps paper clip pencil sticky notes thermometer

1 It's used to hold pieces of paper together. *paper clip*
2 They're used to close different kinds of bottles. ....
3 It's used for writing or drawing. ....
4 It's used to measure a person's temperature. ....
5 They're used to put notes on documents, computers, and other surfaces. ....

REACT

7 Work in groups. Choose the three most useful everyday objects from the photos. Explain your choices.

PHRASE BYTES

I think this is called …
It's used for …
People use it to …

HOW TO

understand new words

- ☐ First, look at any pictures or visuals and read the task. Predict words you might hear.
- ☐ Use familiar words to help you understand the main ideas.
- ☐ Don't stop listening when you hear words you don't understand.

PHRASE BYTES

I think the … is useful because …
The … is more useful than …

MOVE BEYOND

Do the Words & Beyond exercise on page 69.

Workbook, pages 128–129

GRAMMAR Simple past passive

Use the simple past passive to talk about completed actions in the past

READ Grammar in context

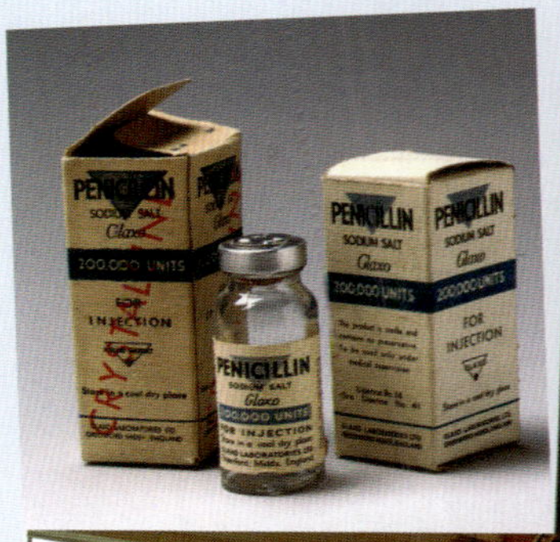

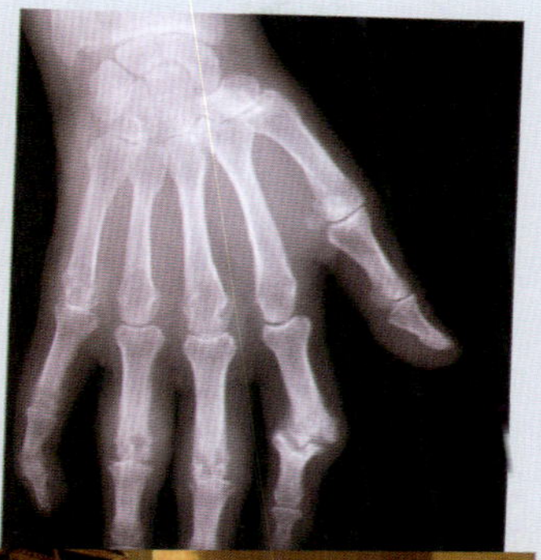

1 Read an article about London's Science Museum. Why does it mention the X-ray machine?

The Science Museum in London was opened in 1909. To celebrate its centenary in 2009, ten objects were chosen from the museum's collection and the public was asked to vote for the invention that changed the future. Penicillin and the Apollo 10 space capsule were both on the list, but they weren't selected. The X-ray machine was voted the number one invention by the public.

STUDY

2 Complete the explanations. Use Exercise 1 to help you.

Simple past passive

Use the passive when the action is more important than the person who does the action.

Affirmative and negative

To form the passive in the simple past tense, use *was* or *were* + (not) + past participle.

The Science Museum in London __________ *opened in 1909.*

Cell phones __________ *invented by Thomas Edison.*

Questions

To form a question in the simple past passive, use: *was, were* + subject + past participle

__________ *penicillin selected? No, it* __________ .

See GRAMMAR DATABASE, page 64.

PRACTICE

3 Complete the sentences with the simple past passive form of the verbs.

1 X-rays *were discovered* (discover) in 1885 by German scientist Wilhelm Conrad Röntgen.
2 The invisible rays created an image when they __________ (project) onto a film.
3 The rays __________ (not stop) by thick paper, or by the bones in his hand.
4 X-rays __________ (first use) in a hospital only two months after their discovery.
5 They __________ (not understand) until later.
6 Röntgen __________ (gave) the first ever Nobel Prize for physics in 1901.

4 Write complete sentences with the simple past passive and the words in the box.

Alexander Fleming	a French artist
~~China~~	physics and chemistry
Tim Berners-Lee	Henry Ford

1 The first rockets / make / in __________
The first rockets were made in China.
2 Marie Curie / give / Nobel prizes in __________
3 The first car for the public / build / by __________
4 Penicillin / discover / by __________
5 The internet / invent / by __________
6 The Statue of Liberty / design / by __________

5 Write the verbs in the active or passive form of the simple past.

In 1969 three astronauts (1) *traveled* (travel) to the moon and (2) __________ (bring) back safely in the Apollo 11 space capsule. The capsule (3) __________ (call) *Columbia*, and it (4) __________ (send) into space on top of the Apollo 11 rocket. When Neil Armstrong and Edwin Aldrin (5) __________ (walk) on the moon on July 20, the moment (6) __________ (see) on TV by 500 million people around the world. The moon walk (7) __________ (also watch) by the third astronaut, Michael Collins. He (8) __________ (have to) stay in the space capsule.

WRITE AND SPEAK

6 a Take the Inventions Quiz. Work in groups of four. Pair A looks at page 71. Pair B looks at page 72. Write sentences using the information.

b Read your sentences to the other pair. Are they correct? Which pair wrote the most correct quiz sentences?

Workbook, page 130

LANGUAGE & BEYOND

$$\Phi(x) = \frac{1}{\sqrt{2\pi\sigma}} e^{\frac{(x-\mu)^2}{2\sigma^2}}$$

Young Inventors Competition

The Science Museum is looking for the inventors of tomorrow. Do you have an original idea? Could you be the next Thomas Edison or Steve Jobs? Enter our Young Inventors Competition to find out.

What to do

The Young Inventors Competition is open to anyone from around the world between the ages of 12 and 17. All you have to do is work in a group and think of an idea for a new invention. Choose from the categories below.

Communication **Environment** **Home** **Crime prevention** **Health & education** **Sports**

If your idea is chosen, you will get the chance to develop your idea at the Science Museum.

››› Share and exchange new ideas

GET THINKING

SPEAK AND READ

1 **Work in pairs. Look at the competition information. Can you take part?**

2 **Which of the categories would you choose and why?**

PHRASE BYTES

I'd choose … or … because …

I think … is the best category because …

Brainstorming **is a way of developing new ideas by talking with several people, making a lot of suggestions, and choosing the best ones. Here are some brainstorming tips.**

- Offer as many ideas as you can.
- Listen to other people's ideas.
- Use other people's ideas to think of new ideas.
- Encourage quiet people to offer ideas.
- Make a list of the different ideas.
- Don't say an idea is good or bad too quickly.
- Don't choose the best idea until you finish brainstorming.

DO

3 **Do you know what brainstorming is? Read the information to the right and check your ideas.**

4 **Work in groups. Brainstorm ideas for the Science Museum competition.**

5 **Choose the best idea and present it to the rest of the class.**

PHRASE BYTES

I have an idea!

How about … ?

We could …

Why don't we … ?

REFLECT

6 **Discuss the questions with your class. Do you agree with the REFLECTION POINT?**

1. Was it easy to choose the category and the best idea for the category? Why or why not?
2. Which of the tips in Exercise 3 did you follow? Are there any you didn't follow? Why?
3. Did you enjoy brainstorming? Did it help you think of new ideas?

REFLECTION POINT

Sharing and exchanging ideas with other people can often help you think of better and more practical ideas.

EXTEND

7 **Work in groups. Brainstorm ideas for a new museum. The museum can be dedicated to anything or anyone of your choice. Give your museum a name and make a list of some of the things people will find there.**

››› Workbook, page 133

SPEAKING At the hardware store

Describe things when you don't know the English word

SPEAK

1 Work in pairs. Look at the picture and answer the questions.

1. What do you see in the picture to the right? What do you need to make this?
2. Have you ever tried to buy something when you didn't know what it was called?
3. What can you do when you're in this situation?

LISTEN

2 58 Listen to the conversation. Which of the things in the pictures (a–f) does Andrew buy to make his kite?

a

b
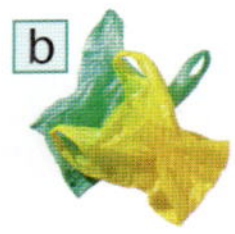
c

d

e

f
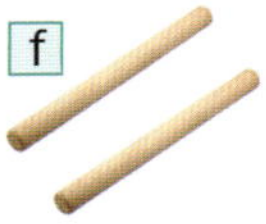

Andrew: Excuse me. I need to buy something like string, but it's used for fishing. I don't know what it's called.
Assistant: I think you mean fishing line.
Andrew: Fishing line, yeah.
Assistant: How much do you need?
Andrew: About 150 meters.
Andrew: Do you have any plastic garbage bags?
Assistant: Small or large?
Andrew: They need to be half a meter wide and one meter long.
Assistant: OK, the small ones. How many boxes would you like?
Andrew: Two boxes, please.
Andrew: I'm not sure what it's called, but it's for sticking things together. It's black, and it's for covering electric cables.
Assistant: You mean this electrical tape?
Andrew: That's it. And I need some long, thin pieces of wood.
Assistant: Oh, you mean sticks.
Andrew: Yes. That's it. How much is everything?
Assistant: That's $32.49.

3 Complete the questions with the question words in the box. Then answer the questions.

How | How big | How many | ~~How much~~ | How much | What kind

1. *How much* fishing line does Andrew want?
2. ______ plastic bags does he buy?
3. ______ do the bags need to be?
4. ______ of tape does he want?
5. ______ does Andrew describe the pieces of wood?
6. ______ does everything cost?

4 a Read the tips in the HOW TO box.

b 59 Complete the excerpts from the conversation. Then listen and repeat.

1. I need to buy something like *string*. I don't know what it's ______.
2. It's used ______ fishing.
3. It's for sticking ______ together. It's ______.

5 Match the phrases in Exercise 4b to the tips in the HOW TO box.

ACT

6 Work in pairs. Do the role play. Then change roles.

Choose an object from Unit 10. Role-play a conversation between a store assistant and a customer. The customer doesn't know the name of the object and has to describe it.

HOW TO

describe things when you don't know the English word

- Say that you don't know the name.
- Call it *a thing* or *something* if it's an object or *stuff* if it's material.
- Say what it's used for.
- Describe it (size, material, color).
- Compare it to something (*it's like … , it's similar to …*).

PHRASEBOOK 60

Describe something you don't know the name of

I don't know / I'm not sure what it's called.
I need something like …
People / You use it for / to …
It's for / like …

Shopping phrases

I need …
Can you show me?
Do you have any … ?
How much is everything / it / that?

Workbook, page 115

WRITING In my opinion

»» Present an argument

SPEAK AND READ

1 **Work in pairs. Look at the photos. What are the things and what do they all have in common?**

2 **Read the essay that Emilio wrote for homework. What question is he answering?**

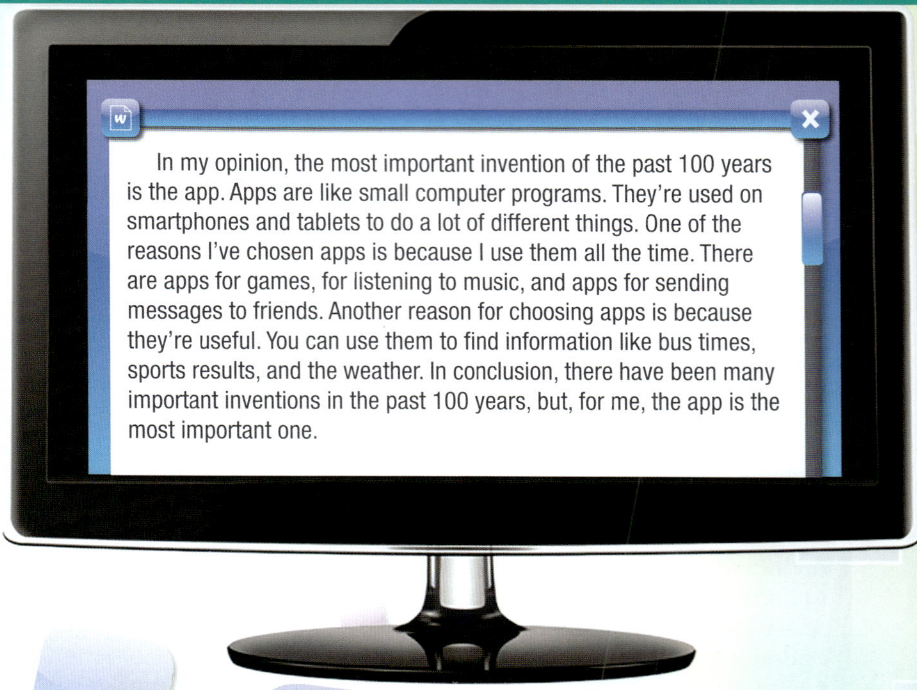

In my opinion, the most important invention of the past 100 years is the app. Apps are like small computer programs. They're used on smartphones and tablets to do a lot of different things. One of the reasons I've chosen apps is because I use them all the time. There are apps for games, for listening to music, and apps for sending messages to friends. Another reason for choosing apps is because they're useful. You can use them to find information like bus times, sports results, and the weather. In conclusion, there have been many important inventions in the past 100 years, but, for me, the app is the most important one.

3 a **Read the tips in the HOW TO box.**

HOW TO

present an argument

- Summarize your argument in the first paragraph.
- Give one or more reasons to support your argument.
- Finish with a conclusion.

b **Underline the phrases Emilio uses for each of the points in the HOW TO box.**

PRACTICE

4 **Match the sentence halves. Then identify the invention.**

1 In my opinion, *c*
2 One of the reasons ___
3 Another reason for ___
4 I use it to do a lot of fun things like ___
5 It also helps me ___
6 In conclusion, ___

a make videos, play music, and draw pictures.
b it can help me study and play.
c the ___ is the most important invention.
d making it my first choice, is it's simple to use.
e do my homework.
f I like it is because it's easy to carry.

DISCUSS

5 **Discuss several important inventions in the last 100 years.**

WRITE

6 **Write about the invention you think is the most important.**

1 Explain why you think the invention is important. Use examples to support your argument. Introduce your argument with these phrases: *in my opinion, one of the reasons, another reason why, another reason for choosing.* See the HOW TO box.

2 Describe the invention. Use the present passive to explain where and when the invention is used.

3 Give some history about the invention. Use the past passive to explain when it was invented and where it was first made.

SHARE

7 **Present your invention to a small group of classmates. Did you choose the same invention? Who gave the best reasons for his or her choice?**

»» Workbook, pages 132–133

VOCABULARY Science verbs and materials

1 Complete the verbs in an ad for a museum.

> **The Museum of**
> **Crazy Creations (MCC)**
>
> Visit the MCC, the museum where you (1) in _ _ _ _ crazy new things and we help you (2) de _ _ _ _ and (3) bu _ _ _ them. Choose from materials such as (4) me _ _ _, (5) pl _ _ _ _ _, (6) gl _ _ _, and (7) st _ _ _, and we'll (8) cr _ _ _ _ a 3D image of your invention. And if we really like your idea, we'll (9) ca _ _ _ _ _ _ _ the amount of material needed and then (10) pr _ _ _ _ _ it.
>
> Come to the MCC. (11) Ex _ _ _ _ _ your imagination and (12) di _ _ _ _ _ _ the crazy ideas in your mind!

___ /12

Everyday objects – *designed by you!*

1 clothes bulb

2 paper cap

3 sticky can

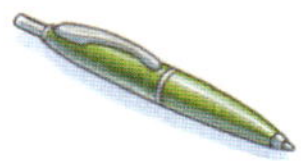
4 ballpoint pin

5 notes

6 light pen

7 thumb clip

8 thermometer

9 bottle tack

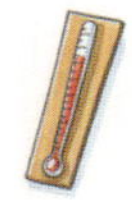
10 pencil

2 The names of the objects in the pictures are all wrong. Write the correct names.

1 .... 6 ....
2 .... 7 ....
3 .... 8 ....
4 .... 9 ....
5 .... 10 ....

___ /10

GRAMMAR Simple present passive

3 Complete the description with the simple present passive form of the verbs.

Specser

This unique device (1) .... (**make**) of plastic, has a microchip inside, and it (2) .... (**put**) on reading glasses. But what do you think (3) .... (**it / use**) for? When you can't find your glasses, you shout "Specser!" and your voice (4) .... (**recognize**) by a microchip inside the device. The Specser then makes a loud beeping sound. Specsers (5) .... (**sell**) in five different colors in our store, and they (6) .... (**not find**) anywhere else in the world!

___ /12

Simple past passive

4 Complete the description with the simple past active or passive form of the verbs.

Coolit

This incredible idea (1) .... (**invent**) by six-year-old Carla Simons. She (2) .... (**have**) her idea in the museum's café. Her hot chocolate (3) .... (**be**) too hot to drink, so she (4) .... (**decide**) that a special machine (5) .... (**need**) to cool it down. Her idea (6) .... (**give**) to us on the back of a menu from the café. We (7) .... (**like**) it so much that the first Coolits (8) .... (**make**) by our engineers just three weeks later.

___ /16

Your score: ___ /50

SKILLS CHECK

✓✓✓ Yes, I can. No problem!
✓✓ Yes, I can. But I need a little help.
✓ Yes, I can. But I need a lot of help.

I can use pictures for help with new words. ....
I can understand new words when I listen. ....
I can share and exchange new ideas. ....
I can describe things when I don't know the English word. ....
I can present an argument when I write. ....

Workbook, pages 134–135

READ

1 Read the article and decide if the sentences are correct (*C*) or incorrect (*I*).

1 Oscar's family got tickets to the Olympics in a lottery. ____
2 Oscar slept well the night before the big day. ____
3 The stadium wasn't built long ago. ____
4 A lot of the materials that were used in the stadium were recycled. ____
5 The security checks at the entrance weren't very strict. ____
6 You could only take drinks in plastic bottles. ____
7 Oscar's sister doesn't like places where there are a lot of people. ____
8 It didn't take very long to get into the stadium. ____
9 The stadium wasn't as big inside as Oscar was expecting. ____
10 Oscar had a very good view of the games. ____

TEST-TAKING TIPS

do a true/false activity

- Read the sentences carefully before you read the text.
- Look at any pictures that can help you understand the text.
- Read the text carefully and choose the correct answers.
- Check details: if any part of the sentence is false, then it's incorrect.

An amazing day

by Oscar Flynn

My family went to see a day of athletics at the London Olympics. We put our names in a lottery with thousands of other people, and our names were chosen! We were really lucky to get tickets. The night before our trip, I was too excited to sleep.

The Olympic Stadium was on a little island, so you had to walk over one of the five bridges to get in. Outside the stadium wasn't as interesting as in photos. It looked like a big bowl. It was completely new – it was built especially for the Olympics. Dad said it took three years to build it, and it cost 500 million pounds. The stadium was designed with different layers and is more environmentally friendly than other stadiums. A big hole was dug in the ground for the bottom layer. All the metal that was used in the top layer of the stadium was recycled, and many of the other materials like stone were recycled from other building projects. I thought that was really cool.

We had to get there two and a half hours before the events started. Everybody's bags and pockets were checked at the entrance. Of course, you couldn't take knives or any other dangerous things. You couldn't take any glass bottles or metal cans or any drinks (you could take empty plastic bottles and fill them with water inside). You also couldn't bring anything that made a loud noise, flags, big umbrellas – or pets! One lady brought a little dog in her bag, and she couldn't go in.

There were long lines of people at the entrance, and we had to wait for a long time. My sister got really stressed because she doesn't like big crowds or places where there isn't open space. She feels like she can't breathe. I was worried and thought, "Oh, no, we'll have to go home," but Dad told her to take deep breaths and stay calm. After a while she felt calm enough, and finally we got inside.

The stadium was much bigger than it looked outside. Our seats were at the top, and we couldn't see much because we were too far away. It was also louder than I expected. People were cheering and screaming and shouting – especially when the big races were on. It was a fantastic feeling to be there with all the other people who were watching. It was an amazing day.

Reading: ______ /10

LISTEN

2 (61) **Listen and check (✓) the correct picture for each question.**

1 What sports equipment does Carlos want to buy?

 A ☐  B ☐  C ☐

2 Which picture shows Alice?

 A ☐  B ☐  C ☐

3 What is Jamie talking about?

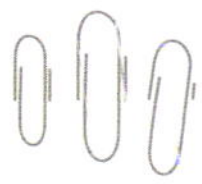 A ☐  B ☐ C ☐

4 What does Fernando want to do?

 A ☐  B ☐  C ☐

5 What time are the students going to go to the museum?

 A ☐  B ☐  C ☐

Listening: ______ /10

TEST-TAKING TIPS

answer multiple-choice questions with pictures

- Read the questions carefully before you listen.
- Look at the pictures: what English words and numbers do they show?
- Predict words you might hear.
- Listen carefully to these words and numbers, and for the main ideas.
- When you listen again, check your answers.

WRITE

3 Complete the second sentence so that it means the same as the first. Use no more than three words.

1 The school chose Paulo's idea for the sports competition.
Paulo's idea ______ for the sports competition.

2 That's Paolo, the one with the orange T-shirt.
Paolo is the one ______ is wearing the orange T-shirt.

3 His idea was more exciting than my idea.
My idea wasn't ______ as his idea.

4 My competition idea was too boring.
My competition idea wasn't interesting ______ .

______ /4

4 Write a message on a forum about your favorite sport (35–45 words).

- Say what the sport is and where you can get information about it.
- Give two reasons why it's a good sport for young people.

______ /6

Writing: ______ /10

Progress check score ______ /30

TEST-TAKING TIPS

write a message

- Read the task carefully. Who are you writing to?
- Plan your message before you write.
- Include phrases to start and end your message.
- Use *because* before a reason and *so* before a result.

Zero conditional

USE

- Use the zero conditional to describe situations that are always true:
  If you eat a balanced diet, your body ***works*** *better.*
  If I exercise a lot, I ***get*** *hungry.*
  You ***can't play*** *tennis if you break your arm.*

FORM

A zero conditional sentence has two parts or "clauses."

- The *if* clause describes the action. Use *if* + simple present verb:
  If you heat water to 100 °C, *it boils.*
- The result clause says what happens. Use a simple present verb:
  If you heat water to 100 °C, ***it boils.***
- Don't use a comma if the result clause comes first:
  It takes six weeks to get better if you break your arm.
  Note: You can also use the imperative or *should* + verb in the result clause. You often use this to give advice:
  If you exercise, ***drink*** *a lot of water.*
  If you burn your hand, you ***should put*** *ice on it.*

should

USE

- Use *should/shouldn't* + verb to say that something is/isn't a good idea:
  If Stefan doesn't feel well, he ***should go*** *to the doctor.*
  You ***should eat*** *more fruit.*
  If you have a headache, you ***shouldn't listen*** *to loud music.*
  If there's a red flag, they ***shouldn't swim*** *in the ocean*

FORM

- *Should* is the same in all forms. Do not add -s to the *he, she,* or *it* form:
  Daisy ***should stay*** *at home if she has a stomachache.* (not ~~*Daisy shoulds*~~ *...*)
- To form questions, use *should* + subject + verb:
  Should he take *the pills in the morning or at night?*
  Should you tell *the teacher about the girl who laughs at you?*
  What ***should I do*** *if I don't feel well?*

First conditional

USE

- Use the first conditional to talk about possible situations in the future and their results:
  If *Rosa works hard, she****'ll pass*** *her exams.*
  If *you make eye contact with the audience, they****'ll listen*** *more carefully.*
  We ***might not finish*** *the fun run* ***if*** *we don't train enough.*

FORM

A first conditional sentence has two parts or "clauses."

- The *if* clause describes the action. You usually use *if* + a simple present verb:
  If Rosa works hard, *she'll pass her exams.*
- The result clause says what will or may happen.
  When you are 100 percent sure, use *will/won't* + verb:
  If Rosa works hard, ***she'll pass her exams.***
  When you are 75 percent sure, use *will probably* + verb:
  If Rosa works hard, ***she'll probably pass her exams.***
  When you are 50 percent sure, use *may/might* or *may not/might not* + verb:
  If Rosa works hard, ***she may pass her exams.***
- Don't use a comma if the result comes first:
  They'll give $20 to charity if you finish the run.
- You can use questions in the result clause in zero and first conditional sentences:
  Does water boil *if you heat it to 100 °C?*
  What will you do *if it rains?*
- Sometimes you can use *should* instead of *will* in first conditional sentences to ask questions or to suggest something:
  Should *I call you if we go to the movies tonight?*
- You can also offer help with *Would you like me to ... :*
  Would you like me to *help you with your homework?*

Must / mustn't, have to / don't have to

USE

must and have to

- Use *must* and *have/has to* + verb to say something is necessary: *To be a pilot you* ***have to pass*** *a lot of exams.*

don't have to

- Use *don't/doesn't* + *have to* + verb to say something isn't necessary: *My mom* ***doesn't have to go*** *to work today.*

mustn't

- Use *mustn't (must not)* + verb to say something is forbidden or dangerous:
You ***mustn't use*** *the elevator if there's a fire.*

WATCH OUT! **Mustn't has a different meaning than don't have to.** *Mustn't* = not allowed: *You* ***mustn't talk*** *in class. Don't have to* = not necessary (but possible): *I* ***don't have to start*** *work early, but sometimes I like to.*

FORM

Affirmative

have to

I/You/We/They	have to	work hard at school.
He/She/It	has to	

must

I/You/He/She/It/We/They	must	arrive on time.

Negative

don't have to

I/You/We/They	don't have to	travel far to school.
He/She/It	doesn't have to	

mustn't

I/You/He/She/It/ We/They	mustn't	eat in class.

Questions and short answers

have to

- Form questions with *do/does* + subject + *have to* + verb.

Questions			Short answers
Do I/you/we/they	have to	work hard?	**Yes**, I/we/they **do**. **No**, I/we/they **don't**.
Does he/she/it			**Yes**, he/she/it **does**. **No**, he/she/it **doesn't**.

Have to, must, and *didn't have to* in the past

- Use *had to* + verb to say something was necessary in the past. Use it for all persons:
I ***had to go*** *to the dentist last week.*
- Use *didn't have to* + verb to say something was not necessary in the past. Use it for all persons: *Malee* ***didn't have to take*** *a test.*
- In questions use *Did (you) have to* + verb:
Did you have to clean *your room on the weekend?*

WATCH OUT! **There is no simple past form of *must*.** **Use *had to / didn't have to*:**
I ***had to*** *stay late at school yesterday.*

Present perfect

USE

Use the present perfect

- to talk about actions in the past when you don't know the exact time or it's not important:
Thomas ***has designed*** *many apps.*
- to talk about experiences you have had up to now:
*I****'ve learned*** *to play the guitar and the piano.*

Been to or gone to?

- *Have/Has been* can sometimes mean *have/has visited* and is used for completed actions.
- Use *been* when someone has gone somewhere and come back:
Lucy ***has been*** *to Spain. She came home last week.*
- Use *gone* when someone has gone somewhere but hasn't come back yet:
Lucy ***has gone*** *to Spain and is still there.*

FORM

Affirmative

- *have/has* + past participle form of the verb.

I/You/We/They	have	**been** to the app club.
He/She/It	has	

Contractions

I**'ve**/You**'ve**/We**'ve**/They**'ve**	**been** to the app club.
He**'s**/She**'s**/It**'s**	

- To form the past participle of regular verbs, add *-ed*:
*design – design**ed***   *help – help**ed***   *start – start**ed***

Note: Sometimes there are spelling changes. These are the same as the spelling changes for the simple past.

See Grammar Database 3 on page 122 for more information.

- Many verbs have irregular past participles. Some of these past participles are the same as the simple past. *(See page 140 for a list of irregular past participles.)*

Negative

- *have/has* + *not* + past participle form of the verb.

I/You/We/They	haven't (have not)	**left** school.
He/She/It	hasn't (has not)	

Questions and short answers

- Form questions in the present perfect with *have* + subject + past participle form of the verb.

Questions			Short answers
Have	I/you/we/they	**been** successful?	**Yes**, I/you/we/they **have**. **No**, I/you/we/they **haven't**.
Has	he/she/it		**Yes**, he/she/it **has**. **No**, he/she/it **hasn't**.

WATCH OUT! **Don't use contractions in affirmative short answers:** *Yes, I have.* (not ~~*Yes, I've.*~~)

Present perfect with *ever* and *never*

- Use the present perfect with *ever* or *never* to talk about experiences you had or didn't have at any time in the past:
  *I've **never seen*** Star Wars.
  ***Have** you **ever been** to a classical concert?*
- Use the present perfect + *ever* to ask if an event happened at any time in the past:
  ***Have** you **ever watched** a wildlife documentary?*
- You usually answer with a short answer:
  *Yes, I **have**. / No, I **haven't**.* *Yes, she **has**. / No, she **hasn't**.*
- Use the present perfect + *never* to say you haven't done something in your life:
  ***I've never written** a blog.*
- Put *ever* before the past participle in questions:
  ***Have** you **ever been** to New York?*
- Put *never* before the past participle in affirmative sentences:
  I've never seen Pirates of the Caribbean.

Present perfect with *already*, *yet*, and *just*

already

- Use the present perfect with *already* for actions completed before now:
  *My dad isn't here. He**'s already gone** to work.*

yet

- Use the present perfect with *yet* in questions to ask if an action is completed or not:
  ***Have** you **seen** the new James Bond movie **yet**? It's terrific!*
- Use the present pefect with *yet* in negative sentences to say an action isn't completed:
  *Bob can't go to the movies tonight because he **hasn't done** his homework **yet**.*

just

- Use the present perfect with *just* for very recent actions:
  ***I've just had** lunch, so I'm not hungry right now.*

WATCH OUT! ***Just*** **and** ***already*** **come before the past participle, but** ***yet*** **comes at the end of the sentence:**
I've just seen *the latest* Star Wars *movie.*
(not ~~*I've seen the latest* Star Wars *movie just*~~.)
***Have** you **done** your math homework **yet**?*
(not ~~*Have you done yet your math homework*~~?)

Present perfect or simple past

- Use the present perfect to talk about things that have happened in the past when you don't know the exact time or the time is not important:
  ***I've told** my mom the truth.*
  ***Have** you **seen** Mike? I don't know where he is.*
- Use the simple past to talk about things that have happened in the past at a specific time:
  ***I told** my mom the secret **yesterday**.* (not ~~*I have told my mom the secret yesterday*~~.)
  ***Did** you **see** the news **last night**?* (not ~~*Have you seen the news last night*~~?)

WATCH OUT! **Don't use the present perfect with specific time expressions (e.g.,** ***last week, yesterday, two years ago, at four o'clock*****). When you include a specific time, use the simple past:**
*We **went** to the United States **last year** for my cousin's birthday.*
(not ~~*We have been to the United States last year for my cousin's birthday*~~.)
Note: You can use the present perfect with phrases relating to unfinished time, such as *this week, this year, today*:
***I've done** a lot of homework **today**, but I didn't do any yesterday.*

- Use the simple past to give other specific details about something that has happened, such as *where, what, who with*:
  A ***Have** you **seen** the new James Bond movie?*
  B *Yes, I **saw** it in Chicago.*
  A ***What did** you **think** of it?*
  B *I **thought** it was terrific!*

Relative clauses

- Use relative clauses to identify or describe people, things, and places:
  *Kids **who play soccer** learn other skills for life.*
  *This sport is popular in Japan **where you can find** the world's biggest bowling alley.*
- Use *that* or *which* for things:
  *Lacrosse and hockey are **sports that** are played with a stick and a ball.*
  *Golf is **a sport that** is played by many older people.*
- Use *who* or *that* for people:
  *That's the **girl who** won the race.*
  *The **player that** most impressed me was the Spanish goalkeeper.*
- Use *where* for places:
  Medellin is the city in Colombia where street soccer began.
  *There are places in **China where** people still make skis from wood and horse skin.*

Comparative and superlative adjectives

USE

- Use comparative adjectives to compare two things:
  *Ben is **older than** Jason, but Ben is faster.*
  *Ice hockey is **more exciting** to watch **than** tennis.*
  *She's **better than** I am at running.*
- Use superlative adjectives to compare one thing with all the others in a group:
  ***The oldest** runner was 101 years old.*
  *That was **the most exciting** race I've ever seen.*
  *In my opinion, he's **the best** player in the world.*

FORM

- To form the comparative of adjectives that have one syllable or two syllables and end in *y*, add *-er*. See the table below for other spelling changes.
- You usually form comparatives with comparative adjective + *than*: *He's a **better** tennis player **than** I am.*
- To form the superlative of adjectives that have one syllable or two syllables and end in *y*, use *the* + adjective + *-est*. See the table below for other spelling changes.

Word type	Adjective	Comparative adjective	Superlative adjective
One syllable	fast	faster	the fastest
One syllable ending in -e	late	later	the latest
One syllable ending in one vowel + one consonant	big	bigger	the biggest
Two syllables ending in -y	busy	busier	the busiest
Two or more syllables	exciting	more exciting	the most exciting
Two or more syllables ending in -ow or -le	narrow	narrower	the narrowest

WATCH OUT! Some comparative and superlative adjectives are irregular:

Adjective	Comparative adjective	Superlative adjective
good	better	the best
bad	worse	the worst
far	farther/further	the farthest/furthest

Note: Put *than* after comparative adjectives when you compare two things in one sentence:
*A golf ball is **heavier than** a table tennis ball.*
You don't need to put *than* if you don't mention the second thing, person, or place:
*This bat is **bigger** and **more useful**.*

Equality and inequality

There are many ways to express equality or inequality when you make comparisons.

less

- *Less* + adjective is the opposite of *more:*
  *I find the geography lessons **less interesting** than the history ones.*
- Only use *less* with adjectives that have more than one syllable.

the least

- *The least* + adjective is the opposite of *the most:*
  *Computer class is my **least favorite** subject at school.*
- Only use *the least* with adjectives that have more than one syllable.

as ... as

- Use *as* + adjective + *as* to say that two things are the same:
  *Rugby is **as popular as** soccer in France.*
- You can use this with all adjectives.

not as ... as

- Use *not as* + adjective + *as* to say that two things are not the same:
  *Table tennis **isn't as exciting as** basketball.*
  *Maya **isn't as fast as** Lia or Rozalia.*
- You can use this with all adjectives.

too and *enough*

- Use *too* before an adjective to mean "more than is necessary or enough":
  *I can't play soccer later. I'm **too tired**.*
- Use *enough* after an adjective to mean "(not) as much as is necessary":
  *Baseball isn't **exciting enough** for me.*

Simple present passive

USE

Use the simple present passive when:

- the action is more important than the person who does the action:
  A cell phone ***is made*** *of plastic and metal.*
  The new designs ***are tested*** *by engineers.*
  What ***is*** *a cell phone* ***made*** *of?*
- the person who does the action is unknown or obvious:
  Every year thousands of cell phones ***are thrown away.***
  Apps ***are used*** *to do a lot of different things.*

- The following sentences mean the same thing:
  Many teenagers ***use*** *cell phones to play games.*
  Cell phones ***are used*** *by many teenagers to play games.*
- The first sentence is active, and the focus is on *Many teenagers*.
- The second sentence is passive, and the focus is on *Cell phones*.

Note: You often find the simple present passive in scientific and technical texts about facts and processes. It is more common in written English than in spoken English.

FORM

Affirmative

- Form the simple present passive with *be* + past participle form of the verb.

It	**is**	**made** of plastic.
They	**are**	**tested** by engineers.

- Use *by* to say who or what does the action:
  New medicines are discovered ***by scientists*** *every year.*
- To form the past participle of regular verbs, add *-ed*:
  *need – need**ed***   *test – test**ed***
  *invent – invent**ed***   *design – design**ed***

WATCH OUT! **Many verbs have irregular past participles. You have to learn these. Some of these past participles are the same as the simple past. (*See page 140 for a list of irregular past participles.*)**

Spelling

Remember that you sometimes have to make spelling changes to regular past participles:

- If a verb ends in *-e*, just add *-d*:
  *recycle – recycle**d***   *use – use**d***
  *celebrate – celebrate**d***
- If a verb ends in *-y*, change the *-y* to *-i* before adding *-ed*:
  *carr~~y~~ – carr**ied***   *tr~~y~~ – tr**ied***
- Don't do this if there is a vowel before the *-y*:
  play – played (not ~~*plaid*~~)
- If a verb ends in one vowel (e.g., *o*) and one consonant (e.g., *p, t*), double the consonant before adding *-ed*:
  *stop – sto**pped***

Negative

- Form the simple present passive negative with *is/are* + *not* + past participle form of the verb:
  Coffee ***isn't grown*** *in California.*
  Cell phones ***aren't recycled*** *enough.*

Questions and short answers

- Form questions in the simple present passive with *Is/Are* + subject + past participle form of the verb:
  Is *your cell phone* ***made*** *of plastic?*
  Yes, *it* ***is.*** */* ***No,*** *it* ***isn't.***
  Are *most cell phones* ***recycled****?*
  Yes, *they* ***are.*** */* ***No,*** *they* ***aren't.***
- You can also use question words (*What, Who, Where, How*) to form questions with the simple present passive:
  How *are the designs chosen?*

Simple past passive

USE

Use the simple past passive when:

- the action is more important than the person who did the action:
  The X-ray machine was voted *the number one invention by the public.*
- the person or thing that did the action is unknown, obvious, or not important:
  The Science Museum in London ***was opened*** *in 1909.*

FORM

Affirmative

- Form the simple past passive with *was/were* + past participle form of the verb:
  The ballpoint pen ***was invented*** *by Lazlo and Georg Biro.*
  Their pens ***are used*** *all around the world.*
- Use *by* to say who or what did the action:
  Penicillin was discovered ***by*** *Alexander Fleming.*

Negative

- Form the simple past passive negative with *was/were* + *not* + past participle form of the verb:
  The can ***wasn't selected*** *to go on the list.*
  X-rays ***weren't discovered*** *until the late 19th century.*

Questions and short answers

- Form questions in the simple past passive with *Was/Were* + subject + past participle of verb:
  Was *the X-ray machine* ***voted*** *the number one invention?*
  Yes, *it* ***was.*** */* ***No,*** *it* ***wasn't.***
  Were *microchips* ***invented*** *in the 19th century?*
  Yes, *they* ***were.*** */* ***No,*** *they* ***weren't.***
- You can also use question words (*What, Who, Where, How*) to form questions with the simple past passive:
  What *was the Apollo 11 space capsule called?*

Page 4

RECALL

PARTS OF THE BODY

arm
back
ear
eye
face
foot
hand
head
leg
mouth
nose
tooth

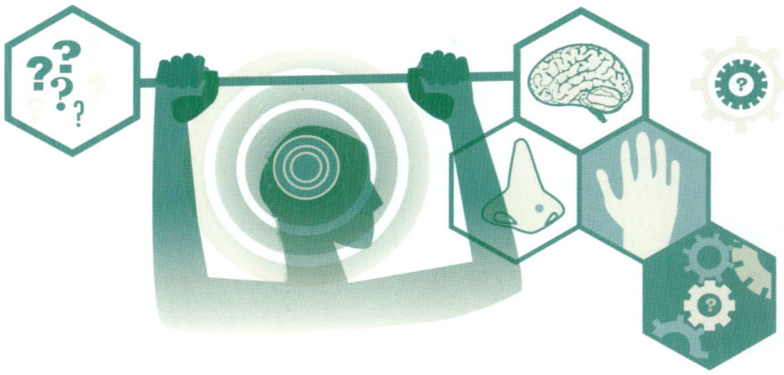

WORK WITH WORDS

TIP: Learn the plural form of nouns. Does the spelling change? Is the plural form different?

TASK: Write the plural form of the RECALL words. Which ones are different?

Pages 4 and 5

PARTS OF THE BODY

ankle
brain
chest
finger
heart
knee
neck
shoulder
stomach
throat
thumb
toe

MOVE BEYOND

Write words you associate with five of the body parts – e.g., verbs, adjectives, clothes. For example, brain: *head, think, intelligent, gray*.

Page 8

EXERCISE VERBS

hold
look down
look up
point
pull
sit down
stand up
stretch
touch
turn

MOVE BEYOND

Choose five verbs. Write an example of when you do the actions. For example, *I* hold *my phone when I use it*.

1 Verb: ....

2 Verb: ....

3 Verb: ....

4 Verb: ....

5 Verb: ....

OTHER IMPORTANT WORDS

audience
backache
balanced
bone
burn (v)
cold (n)
complex
cough (n)
destroy
equal
eye contact
flag
fun run
headache
hurt
hurt yourself
out of shape
pass
puzzle
race (n)
runny nose
sore throat
stomachache
sunscreen
temperature
universe
whole

Page 16

RECALL

JOBS AND WORKPLACES

farmer	farm
doctor, nurse	hospital
receptionist	hotel
cook, waiter/waitress	restaurant
teacher	school
store clerk	store/shopping center

WORK WITH WORDS

TIP: Learn words with related words – for example, jobs and workplaces.

TASK: Make cards with jobs and workplaces. Turn over a job and a workplace. Are they related – can the person work there? If the answer is yes, keep the cards.

Pages 16 and 17

JOBS

artist
cleaner
dentist
driver
engineer
fitness trainer
hairdresser
journalist
mechanic
pilot
secretary
travel agent

WORKPLACES

factory
garage
gym
hair salon
office
travel agency

MOVE BEYOND

1. **Which jobs on the word list do you find interesting? Check (✔) them. Which jobs aren't for you? Cross (✘) them out.**
2. **You can add *-er* to some verbs to make jobs. Make a list of jobs with *-er* from the RECALL box and this list. Write the verbs for the jobs.**

....

....

....

Page 20

WORK AND STUDY

business
career
class
college
company
degree
exams
full-time job
part-time job
school year

MOVE BEYOND

Read the words silently in your head and practice pronunciation. Which word…

… has a silent letter?

… has stress on the third syllable?

… has three syllables with the stress on the first syllable?

OTHER IMPORTANT WORDS

achieve
apology
crocodile
cruel
cut (v)
dangerous
death
design (v)
develop
developer
entertain
equipment
fix
never mind
on time
risk (v)
successful
support (v)

Page 26

RECALL

THINGS WE LISTEN TO
a CD
music
a podcast
the radio

THINGS WE WATCH
a DVD
a movie
television
a TV show
a video

THINGS WE READ
a book
a comic book
a magazine
a newspaper
a website

WORK WITH WORDS

TIP: Use media to help you practice English. Listen to songs, watch movies, and read books, comic books, and websites in English.

TASK: Write down the titles of three songs, three movies, and three books in English.

Pages 26 and 27

KINDS OF MOVIES AND TV SHOWS
action/adventure
cartoon
comedy
documentary
horror
science fiction
western

TV SHOWS ONLY
cooking show
game show
news
talk show
weather

MOVE BEYOND
Think of the title of a movie or TV show for each of the words on the list.

1 ....
2 ....
3 ....
4 ....
5 ....
6 ....
7 ....
8 ....
9 ....
10 ....
11 ....
12 ....

Page 30

CRIME
accident
ambulance
arrest (v)
crime
criminal
police car
police officer
steal (v)
thief
victim

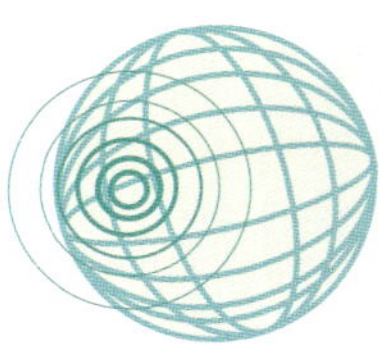

MOVE BEYOND
Write five sentences. Each sentence must contain two different words from the Crime list.

1 ....
2 ....
3 ....
4 ....
5 ....

OTHER IMPORTANT WORDS
action figures
atmosphere
blockbuster
board games
character
chopsticks
delay (n)
ending
episode
galaxy
genre
guest
influence (n)
karaoke
merchandise
rating
results
series
summary
symbol
traffic

WORDS & BEYOND

Page 38

RECALL

BALL SPORTS
baseball
basketball
bowling
(field) hockey
golf
soccer
table tennis
tennis
volleyball

WATER SPORTS
sailing
surfing
swimming

WINTER SPORTS
ice hockey
ice skating
skiing
snowboarding

OTHER
bike riding
dancing
gymnastics
horseback riding
running
skateboarding

WORK WITH WORDS

TIP: Learn the correct verbs for sports. Use *play* for most ball or team sports, *go* for *-ing* sports, and *do* for some other sports.

TASK: Write the correct verbs next to the words on the list above.

Pages 38 and 39

SPORTS EQUIPMENT
- bat ☐
- flippers ☐
- goal ☐
- helmet ☐
- hoop ☐
- mask ☐
- net ☐
- paddle ☐
- puck ☐
- racket ☐
- skates ☐
- snorkel ☐
- stick ☐

MOVE BEYOND
Check (✔) the sports equipment that you or your family have at home.

Page 42

-ED AND *-ING* ADJECTIVES

amazed	amazing
annoyed	annoying
bored	boring
depressed	depressing
disappointed	disappointing
embarrassed	embarrassing
excited	exciting
interested	interesting
relaxed	relaxing
worried	worrying

MOVE BEYOND
1 **Circle the words that describe you now.**
2 **Choose three *-ing* adjectives. Write true sentences about you.**

1 ....
2 ....
3 ....

OTHER IMPORTANT WORDS
breathe
coach (n)
concentrate
court (n)
determined
fair play
fan
field
generous
goal
iron (adj)
keep calm
leather
lucky
mad
pack of cards
referee
score (n)
stressed
violence
wealthy

Page 48

RECALL

PLACES IN A MUSEUM

coffee shop
elevator
entrance
first floor
gift shop
information desk
restrooms
stairs
ticket office

WORK WITH WORDS

TIP: Note words that are different in American and British English.

TASK: Match these British English words to words in RECALL: *ground floor, lift, toilets.*

Pages 48 and 49

SCIENCE VERBS

build
calculate
create
design
develop
discover
explore
invent
produce

MATERIALS

glass
metal
plastic
stone
wood

MOVE BEYOND

Write four sentences using at least one invention verb and one material.

1 ....
2 ....
3 ....
4 ....

Page 52

EVERYDAY OBJECTS

ballpoint pen
bottle cap
can
clothespin
light bulb
paper clip
pencil
sticky notes
thermometer
thumbtack

MOVE BEYOND

Complete with the missing words (or parts of words) without looking at the list:

.... *bulb*
.... *cap*
.... *cil*
.... *clip*
.... *meter*
.... *notes*
.... *pin*
.... *pen*
.... *tack*

OTHER IMPORTANT WORDS

antenna
base station
bones
cell phone
chemist
chemistry
encourage
frequency
heat (n)
ink
microchip
network (n)
newspaper editor
ray
signal (n)
space capsule
string
telescope

IRREGULAR VERBS

base verb	simple past	past participle
be	was/were	been
beat	beat	beaten
become	became	become
begin	began	begun
blow	blew	blown
break	broke	broken
bring	brought	brought
build	built	built
buy	bought	bought
choose	chose	chosen
come	came	come
cost	cost	cost
cut	cut	cut
deal	dealt	dealt
do	did	done
draw	drew	drawn
drink	drank	drunk
drive	drove	driven
eat	ate	eaten
fall	fell	fallen
feed	fed	fed
feel	felt	felt
fight	fought	fought
find	found	found
fly	flew	flown
forget	forgot	forgotten
get	got	gotten
give	gave	given
go	went	gone
grow	grew	grown
hang (out)	hung (out)	hung (out)
have	had	had
hear	heard	heard
hit	hit	hit
hold	held	held
hurt	hurt	hurt
keep	kept	kept

base verb	simple past	past participle
know	knew	known
lay	laid	laid
leave	left	left
lose	lost	lost
make	made	made
mean	meant	meant
meet	met	met
overtake	overtook	overtaken
pay	paid	paid
put	put	put
read	read	read
ride	rode	ridden
ring	rang	rung
run	ran	run
say	said	said
see	saw	seen
sell	sold	sold
send	sent	sent
shine	shone	shone
sing	sang	sung
sit	sat	sat
sleep	slept	slept
speak	spoke	spoken
spend	spent	spent
stand	stood	stood
steal	stole	stolen
swim	swam	swum
take	took	taken
teach	taught	taught
tell	told	told
think	thought	thought
throw	threw	thrown
understand	understood	understood
wake up	woke up	woken up
wear	wore	worn
win	won	won
write	wrote	written

STUDENT A

UNIT 8 IN THE PICTURE

Page 27, Exercise 7

TV survey

1. How many televisions are there in your home?
2. How many hours of television do you normally watch each day?
3. What's your favorite TV channel?
4. How often do you watch these kinds of shows – rarely, occasionally, or often?

cooking shows	game shows
documentaries	talk shows
the news	the weather

UNIT 10 GRAMMAR 2

Page 53, Exercise 6a

Invention/ discovery	Verb	By	Date
The telephone		Levi Strauss	1924
Frozen food		Eugene Polley	1876
Blue jeans	invent	Charles Birdseye	1955
The TV remote control		Alexander Graham Bell	1853

Answers for pair B:
Bubble gum was invented by Walter E. Diemer in 1928.
The radio was invented by Guglielmo Marconi in 1895.
Coca-Cola® was invented by John Pemberton in 1886.
The cell phone was invented by Martin Cooper in 1973.

ANSWERS

UNIT 6 READING

Page 6, Exercise 5

Puzzle answers

1. Second place
2. 21. You multiply by 2 and subtract 1.
3. Short
4. Tuesday, Thursday, today, and tomorrow
5. If you take away two letters, the first and the last, you have IV. This is 4 in Roman numerals.

UNIT 9 GRAMMAR

Page 41, Exercise 4b

Sports facts answers

1. 2.31
2. 11
3. olive oil
4. table tennis
5. moon
6. 1–0

UNIT 10 IN THE PICTURE

Page 49, Exercise 8

Science quiz answers

1. **B** Thomas Edison
2. **B** 1969
3. **C** 320 meters
4. **A** The Stone Age

UNIT 8 IN THE PICTURE

Page 27, Exercise 7

Movie survey

1 When did you last go to the movies?

2 Do you prefer to watch movies at the movie theater, on TV, or online?

3 What is your favorite movie right now?

4 What kinds of movies do you prefer? Order them from your most (1) to your least (6) favorite.

action/adventure
horror
cartoon
the news
comedy
science fiction
western
the weather

UNIT 10 GRAMMAR 2

Page 53, Exercise 6a

Invention/ discovery	Verb	By	Date
Bubble gum		John Pemberton	1895
The radio		Guglielmo Marconi	1886
Coca-Cola®	invent	Martin Cooper	1973
The cell phone		Walter E. Diemer	1928

Answers for pair A:
The telephone was invented by Alexander Graham Bell in 1876.
Frozen food was invented by Charles Birdseye in 1924.
Blue jeans were invented by Levi Strauss in 1853.
The TV remote control was invented by Eugene Polley in 1955.

Posters

LANGUAGE & BEYOND

Page 44, Exercise 6

Move Beyond 4

WORKBOOK

macmillan education

Nina Lauder
Ingrid Wisniewska

Macmillan Education
4 Crinan Street
London N1 9XW
A division of Macmillan Publishers Limited

Companies and representatives throughout the world

ISBN 978-1-380-00775-9

Written by Nina Lauder and Ingrid Wisniewska

Go Beyond First published 2015
First edition entitled *Beyond* published 2014

Designed by EMC Design Ltd.

Illustrated by Peter Cornwell p. 124; Cyrus Deboo p. 77; Stephen Dew pp. 79, 134; Mark Duffin p. 88; Kevin Hopgood pp. 81, 84, 105, 114; Bob Lea p. 76 (cr); Roger Stewart (Beehive Illustration) p. 104; Tony Wilkins pp. 76 (bl), 80, 125.

Cover design by EMC Design Ltd.
Cover photograph by Getty Images/F1online/parasola parasola
Picture research by Tessa Hammond and Emily Taylor

The authors and publishers would like to thank the following for permission to reproduce their images:

Alamy/Michael Flippo/Sports Images p. 112(1), Alamy/Lamb p. 129(1), Alamy/Oleksandr Perepelytsia p. 131(a), Alamy/PhotoEdit p. 112(7), Alamy/Radius Images p. 107, Alamy/Doug Steley p. 128(b), Alamy/Studiomode p. 106, Alamy/Gregg Vignal p. 89(tl), Alamy/Stacy Walsh Rosenstock p. 120;
Brand X p. 131(bm);
Corbis/Eric Audras/PhotoAlto p. 132, Corbis/Johnny Franzen/Johner Images p. 128(c), Corbis/Vladimir Godnik/Beyond p. 90(inset), Corbis/Hufton & Crow/View p. 130, Corbis/Igor E./Image Source p. 123, Corbis/KidStock/Blend Images p. 92, Corbis/John Lund/Blend Images p. 119(c), Corbis/Tim Mannakee/SOPA p. 101, Corbis/Lawrence Manning p. 112(6), Corbis/Motofish Images p. 90(b), Corbis/Sol Neelman p. 113(tr), Corbis/Ocean p. 89(bl), Corbis/Radius Images p. 83, Corbis/RelaXimages p. 77(r), Corbis/Jeff Vanuga p. 100, Corbis/Hideki Yoshihara/Aflo p. 128(d);
FotoLibra/Darryl Brooks p. 128(a);
Getty Images p. 112(4), Getty Images/Carlos Alvarez p. 129(6), Getty Images/Cultura/Luc Beziat p. 119(b), Getty Images/Howard Shooter p. 131(b), Getty Images/E+ p. 99, Getty Images/Richard Newstead/Moment Open p. 129(4), Getty Images/Jules Frazier/Photodisc p. 112(2), Getty Images/Ragnar Schmuck p. 129(3), Getty Images/Fuse p. 131(d), Getty Images/Christopher Futcher p. 119(a), Getty Images/Image Source p. 77(l), Getty Images/Sean Justice p. 117, Getty Images/Jonathan Kantor p. 131(c), Getty Images/Ron Levine p. 93, Getty Images/Pascal Preti p. 116, Getty Images/Photodisc/Derek Latta p. 77(m), Getty Images/Tim Robberts/Digital Vision p. 80, Getty Images/Tunart p. 96;
ImageSource p. 129(5);
Rex Features/Nigel Howard/Associated Newspapers p. 113(bl), Rex Features/Eddie Mulholland p. 115;
Science Photo Library p. 119(a);
Thinkstock/Hemera Technologies p. 112(8), Thinkstock/iStock pp. 112(3, 5), 129(2).

Commissioned photographs by Studio8 Ltd., p. 81

Printed and bound in China

2021 2020 2019 2018 2017
10 9 8 7 6 5 4 3 2 1

CONTENTS

6 UNIT MIND AND BODY

VOCABULARY 1 >>> Parts of the body

1 a Find six parts of the body using the code.

	1	2	3	4
A	c	r	s	e
B	h	a	f	k
C	b	i	o	l
D	t	g	n	m

(e.g., A1 = c C3 = o)

1 D1 / C3 / A4 ......*toe*......
2 B4 / D3 / A4 / A4 ....
3 D3 / A4 / A1 / B4 ....
4 D1 / B1 / A2 / C3 / B2 / D1 ....
5 B1 / A4 / B2 / A2 / D1 ....
6 A1 / B1 / A4 / A3 / D1 ....

b Think of two more parts of the body.

....

2 a Label the picture with the correct parts of the body.

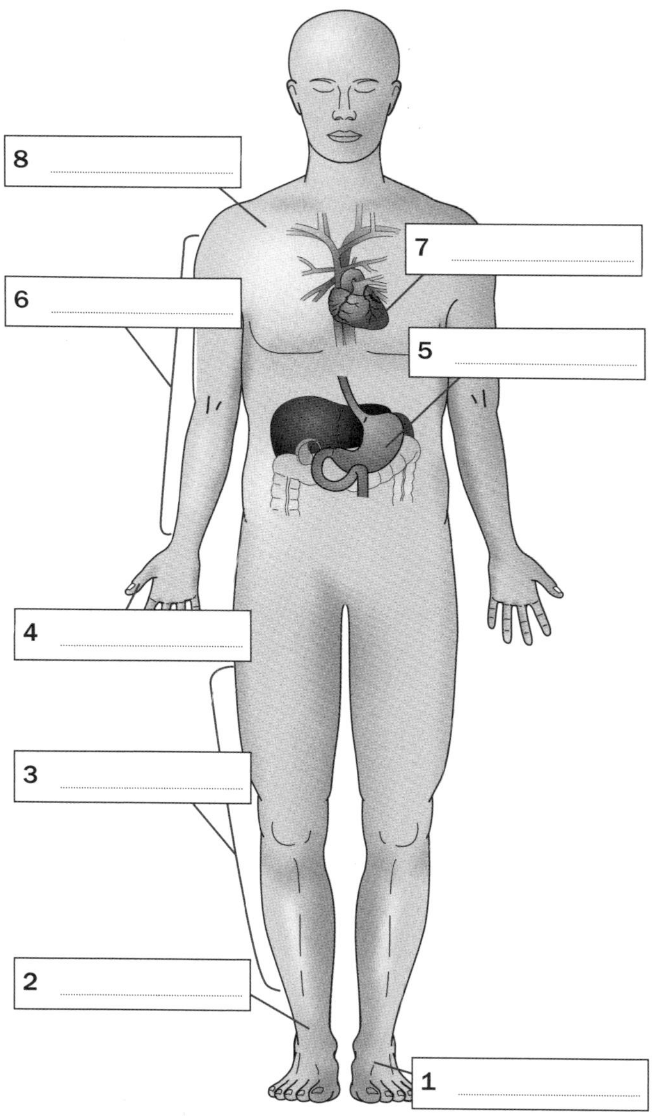

b Label two more parts of the body.

3 Match the parts of the body (1–6) to the places (a–f) where you find them.

1 toe
2 heart
3 eye
4 thumb
5 knee
6 tooth

a mouth
b foot
c hand
d face
e leg
f chest

4 Complete the questions about the avatar.

1 Q: Does it have two .... ?
A: No, it has one.
2 Q: Does it have eight .... ?
A: Yes, it does.
3 Q: Does it have a big round .... ?
A: Yes, it does.
4 Q: Does it have many .... ?
A: No, it only has two.
5 Q: Does it have three .... ?
A: Yes, it does.
6 Q: Does it have six .... ?
A: Yes, it does.

5 Write the words in the correct circles.

ankle back chest ear eye
toe knee mouth shoulder

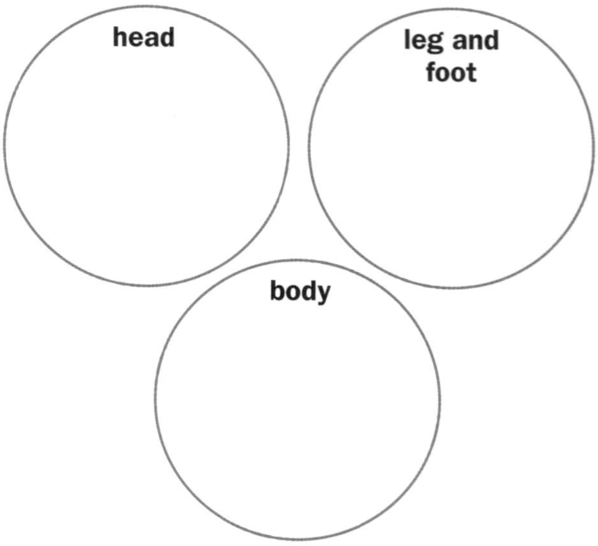

Read quickly

1 Label the activities.

1  ch ______

2 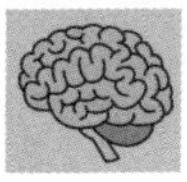 br ______ - ______ games

3  ex ______

4  cr ______ s

5 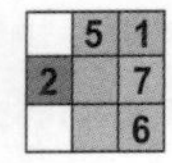

S ______

2 Find and underline the activities from Exercise 1 in the texts. Try to find them all in 30 seconds.

Sarah

Personally, I love doing brain-training games like number puzzles and quizzes. I download Sudoku apps onto my cell phone, so I can play them on the bus on the way to school. I don't think they make you more intelligent – they're just fun! My brother loves playing chess, but I hate it. I think it's too complicated and slow.

Tim

Our teacher says that doing crosswords and brain-training games is good for your brain, and that puzzles help us become more intelligent, but in my opinion, they're really boring. I don't think they can make you more intelligent, because they're too difficult to begin with! I prefer real exercise like basketball.

Rob

I really like doing crosswords and Sudoku. I'm also good at playing chess. I play online chess with my cousin every week, and I usually win! Sarah hates playing chess with me because she finds it difficult. I think puzzles are relaxing, and they can help us use our brains better.

REMEMBER HOW TO ...

read quickly

don't groups individual stop word words

- Read (1) ______ of (2) ______ , not (3) ______ words.
- (4) ______ (5) ______ if you don't understand a (6) ______ or sentence.

3 Complete the above tips for reading quickly with the words in the box.

4 a What do/don't Sarah, Tim, and Rob like doing? Complete the table with *like* (L), *don't like* (DL), or *don't know* (DK).

	chess	crosswords	brain-training games	Sudoku
Sarah				
Tim				
Rob				

b Do you think that brain-training games make you more intelligent?

______

5 Read the texts again and answer the questions. Write *Sarah*, *Tim*, or *Rob* next to the sentences (1–6).

1 Who does puzzles on the bus? ______
2 Who thinks brain-training games are hard? ______
3 Who thinks chess is too difficult? ______
4 Who likes playing a type of board game online? ______
5 Who likes playing a ball game? ______
6 Who thinks puzzles are relaxing? ______

MOVE BEYOND

Find and complete a puzzle or word game online. What game did you find? Did you find it easy/difficult/fun?

______

______

GRAMMAR 1 Zero conditional, *should*

>>> Talk about results and the best thing to do

1 Choose the correct option to complete the grammar tables.

Zero conditional sentences		
Action – *If* + simple present		Result – simple present
If	you (1) ***use*** / ***used*** your brain to do puzzles,	you (2) ***are becoming*** / ***become*** more intelligent.
	you don't (3) ***eat*** / ***are eating*** well,	you (4) ***get*** / ***'re getting*** sick.
	you (5) ***want*** / ***wanting*** to get in shape,	you should (6) ***get*** / ***gotten*** more exercise.

should/shouldn't + verb			
Subject	*should/shouldn't*	Main verb	
He	should	(7) ***get*** / ***getting*** more exercise.	
They	shouldn't	(8) ***to smoke*** / ***smoke***.	
Question form			Short answers
Should	Subject	Verb	
Should	he	go to the hospital?	Yes, he (9) ***should*** / ***shouldn't***. No, he (10) ***should*** / ***shouldn't***.

2 Choose the correct option to complete the rules (1–4). Use the table in Exercise 1 to help you.

1 Use zero conditionals to describe things that are always ***true*** / ***false***.
2 Use ***should*** / ***shouldn't*** + verb to say that something is a good idea.
3 Use ***should*** / ***shouldn't*** + verb to say that something is a bad idea.
4 Sometimes use *should* in the ***result*** / ***if*** clause of a zero conditional sentence.

3 Match the sentence halves to complete the zero conditional sentences.

1 If you eat oranges,
2 If you don't get good grades at school,
3 If you do brain-training games and puzzles,
4 If you want to have a healthy heart,
5 If you're a friendly person,
6 If you don't want to feel tired,

a you become more intelligent.
b it's easy to make friends.
c you should sleep at least seven hours a night.
d you should exercise at least three times a week.
e it's hard to get a good job.
f you don't get so many colds.

4 Read the poster below. Complete the sentences with *should* or *shouldn't*.

To stay
HEALTHY ...

1 you ________ sleep well.
2 you ________ have a balanced diet.
3 you ________ smoke.
4 you ________ drink a lot of soft drinks or eat a lot of fast food.
5 you ________ get regular exercise.
6 you ________ drink water every day.

5 › **Look at the signs (1–6). For each sign, write what you should or shouldn't do using a word from the box.**

1

2

3

4

5

6

~~leave your car here~~ put trash here smoke swim use cell phones walk on the grass

1 *You should leave your car here.*
2 ______
3 ______
4 ______
5 ______
6 ______

6 › **Put the words in the correct order to make zero conditional sentences.**

1 If / shouldn't / you / are / you / eat / bread / allergic to / flour .
If you are allergic to flour, you shouldn't eat bread.
2 hear / should / "pardon" / say / If / don't / something / you / you .
______
3 meet / If / I / always say / him / on the street / I / "hello" .
______
4 good / ride our bikes / If / to school / we / the weather / is .
______
5 play basketball / If / you / a fever / shouldn't / have / you .
______
6 there's / If / a red flag / shouldn't / you / swim / on the beach .
______
7 If / he / in the evenings / any / watches / TV / have / doesn't / homework / he .
______
8 worried / gets / late / home / Her mom / gets / she / if .
______

7 ›› **Complete the sentences with the correct form of the verbs in the box.**

boil break go get make mix need not need not switch off rain take waste

1 If you ______ your finger, it usually ______ five weeks to get better.
2 If you ______ red and yellow paint, you ______ orange paint.
3 If you ______ water, it ______ hot.
4 If you ______ the lights when you leave the room, you ______ energy.
5 If it ______, you ______ to wear sunscreen.
6 Do I ______ to wear a sweatshirt if I ______ outside?

8 ››› **Rewrite the sentences using *if* and *should* or *shouldn't*.**

1 You need to study more to get better grades.
If you want to get better grades, you should study more.
2 It's not a good idea to stand under a tree during a storm.
If there's ______
3 You need to exercise to stay healthy.
______
4 Don't use the elevator when there's a fire in the building.
______
5 When it's sunny, always use sunscreen.
______
6 When you have a fever, it's not a good idea to go to school.
______

LISTENING

Understand spoken instructions

1 (62) **Listen and number the activities in the correct order.**

a
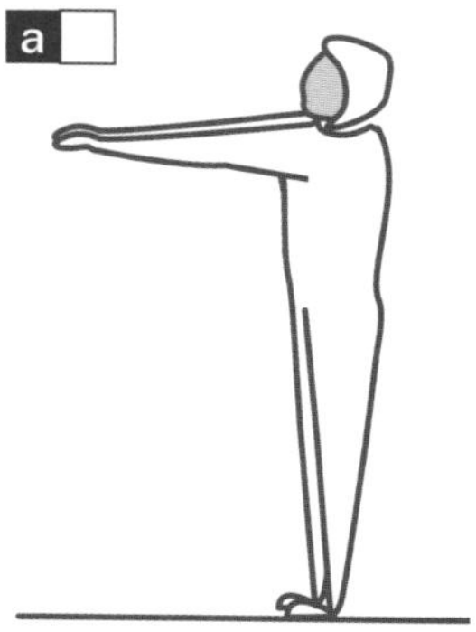

b

c

d 1
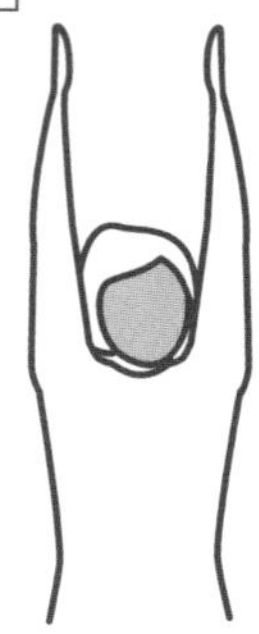

e
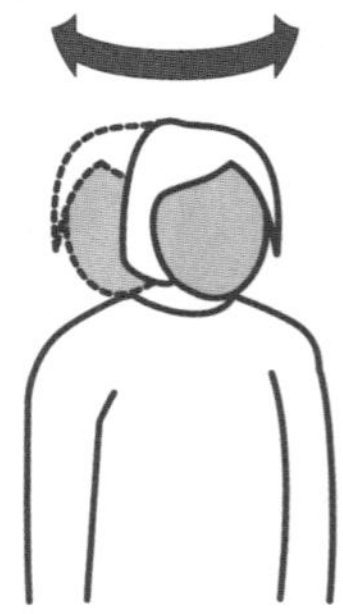

2 Complete the tips with the words in the box.

REMEMBER HOW TO …

understand spoken instructions

adverbs imperatives sequencers

- Listen for (1) .... (*listen, don't talk*). They give instructions.
- Listen for (2) .... (*first, next, then, now*). They tell you when a new instruction starts.
- Listen for (3) .... (*slowly, carefully*). They tell you how to do something.

3 (62) **Listen again and decide if these statements are correct (*C*) or incorrect (*I*).**

1. Alison goes to the gym a lot. ......
2. She doesn't know how to use the gym equipment. ......
3. Carlos is the gym instructor. ......
4. Carlos tells Alison how to warm up. ......
5. Alison says that stretching is boring. ......
6. Alison says she's tired after the warm-up. ......

4 (63) **Complete Carlos's instructions with the words in the box. Then listen and check.**

finally point slowly stand
stretch look touch

1. First .... up straight and .... your arms above your head.
2. .... to the ceiling.
3. Look up, ... down.
4. Next .... turn your head from side to side.
5. Now .... your toes.
6. .... sit down on the floor.

VOCABULARY 2

Exercise and health

1 Read the clues and complete the crossword.

Across

2 L____ u__ to the ceiling, then down at the floor.
3 OK, s_____ u__ from your chair …
5 T____ your body from left to right.
6 Don't r_____ yet. We're not finished!

Down

1 H____ this heavy ball and stretch your arms out.
3 Touch your toes to st______h your back.
4 P____ your left knee up to your chest.
5 T_____ your right knee with your left hand.

2 Complete the text with the correct verbs.

look down   look up   point   sit down   stand up   stretch   touch

TIPS & ADVICE

Before I go swimming, I always (1) __________ . This is my simple stretching routine:
5 x (2) __________ and then (3) __________ slowly, to relax my neck.
5 x (4) __________ and then (5) __________ slowly, to stretch my legs and back.
10 x (6) __________ my ankles – left hand to right ankle, then right hand to left ankle.
15 x (7) __________ my fingers and my toes straight … then get in the pool.

3 Choose the correct option to complete the sentences.

1 While I was making soup, I ***burned*** / ***cooked*** my finger on the saucepan.
2 There are 27 ***bones*** / ***pieces*** in the human hand.
3 Stretch before exercise or you might hurt ***yourself*** / ***you***.
4 My family is doing a local ***fun run*** / ***exercise*** for charity.
5 You should put on ***clothes*** / ***sunscreen*** at the beach.
6 Don't swim in the ocean! There's a ***red flag*** / ***lifeguard*** at the beach.

WORDS & BEYOND

Label the pictures with the symptoms.

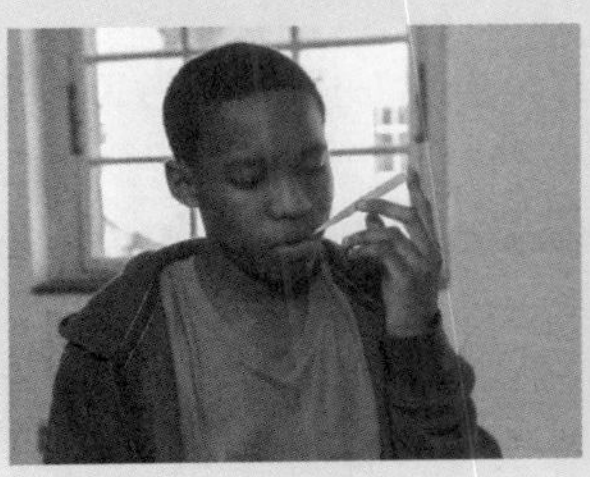

1 a t__p__a__e

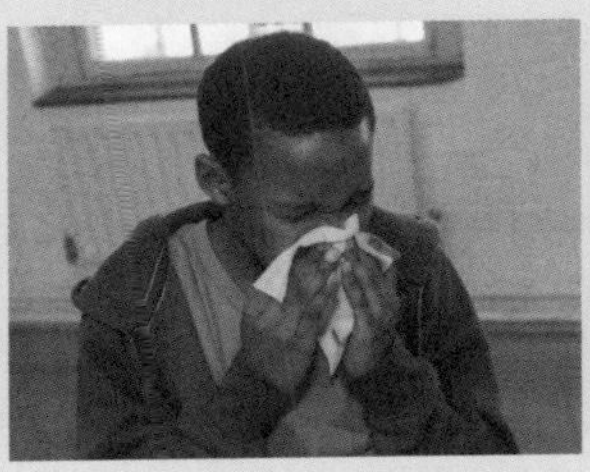

2 a r____y n____

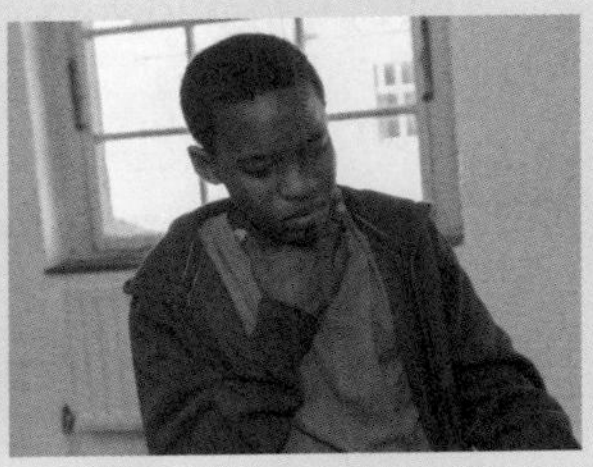

3 a s__e th____t

4 a h____ac____

5 a c____h

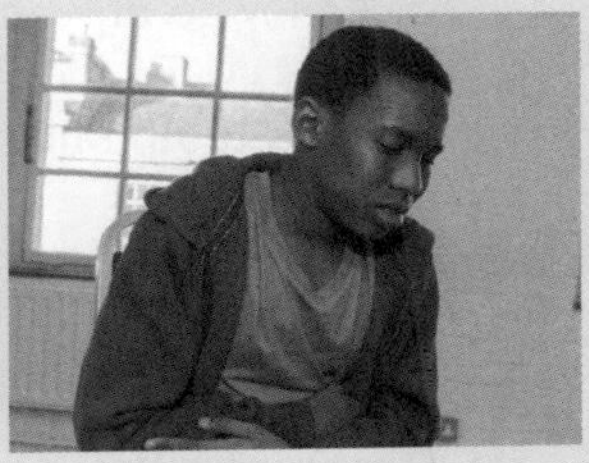

6 a st____ha__e

GRAMMAR 2 First conditional

Talk about possible situations in the future

1 › Choose the correct option to complete the grammar table.

First conditional sentences		
Action – *If* + simple present		Result – *will (probably)* / *(probably) won't* / *may* / *might*
If	he (1) *'s finishing* / *finishes* the race,	they (2) *'re* / *'ll* give $20 to charity.
	you (3) *don't* / *won't* wear good running shoes,	you (4) *'ll* / *'re* hurt yourself.
	we (5) *eat* / *ate* well,	we'll **probably** live longer.
	it (6) *rains* / *was raining* this evening,	I **might** go to the movies.

2 › Choose the correct option to complete the rules. Use the table in Exercise 1 to help you.

1 Use first conditionals when the result of a condition is in the *future* / *present*.
2 Use *will* (*probably*), *may*, or *might* in the *action* / *result* clause.

3 › Write *If* clauses using the prompts. Then match them to the results (a–f).

1 we / not find / a taxi soon
If we don't find a taxi soon, we'll miss our plane.
2 it / start / raining
....
3 it / be / hot
....
4 you / not visit me / later today
....
5 you / not go to bed /early
....
6 you / finish / the race
....

a we'll open the windows.
b we won't need to water the plants.
c you'll be tired.
d I'll give $5 to charity.
e I'll send you a text message tomorrow.
f we'll miss our plane.

4 ›› Write the correct form of the verb in parentheses to complete the sentences.

1 If you *don't study* (not study) hard, you .... (probably not get) good grades.
2 If you .... (not stretch) before you exercise, you might .... (hurt) yourself.
3 If you .... (stay) in bed, you .... (probably feel) better.
4 If she .... (pass) her exams, she .... (definitely be) very happy.
5 If he .... (not finish) his project, his teacher .... (probably give) him a low grade.
6 If he .... (not train) hard, he .... (probably not get) on the team.

5 ››› Write the questions for these answers. Use the prompts in parentheses.

1 Q: *What will you do if it rains?* (What / do?)
A: If it rains, we'll go to the movies.
2 Q: .... (What / study?)
A: If I go to college, I'll study English.
3 Q: .... (Where / go?)
A: If they go on vacation, they'll go to Peru.
4 Q: .... (What / do?)
A: If his tooth still hurts tomorrow, he'll go to the dentist.
5 Q: .... (How much / give?)
A: If she finishes the run, I'll give her $100.
6 Q: .... (Who / meet?)
A: If we go out tonight, we'll meet Sally and Paul.

6 ››› Complete the sentences for you using the first conditional.

If it rains on the weekend, ...
If I get bad grades, ...
If it's hot and sunny tomorrow, ...

Ask for and understand advice at the doctor's office

1 Look at the photo. What do you think is wrong with Megan?

a a backache
b a stomachache
c a headache

2 a 64 Complete the conversation with the words in the box. Then listen and check.

have hurts probably should sore throat What

Dad: What's wrong, Megan?
Megan: I feel terrible, Dad! I (1) ________ a stomachache, my head (2) ________ , and I have a (3) ________ .
Dad: Your face feels hot. You (4) ________ have a fever.
Megan: (5) ________ should I do?
Dad: You need to take a pain reliever and go back to bed.
Megan: But I can't miss school today. I have practice for the school play.
Dad: I don't think you (6) ________ go to school. I'll call your teachers to get your homework for today.

b Name two other symptoms you can think of.

________ , ________

3 Number the conversation at the doctor's office in the correct order.

___ Well, not tomorrow, but you'll probably be better by the weekend.
___ And what should I take for my headache?
___ What should I do?
___ I think you should drink a lot of water and rest.
___ You need to take a pain reliever every four hours.
___ Yes, I can see that. I'm afraid you have the flu.
___ Will I be better tomorrow?
_1_ Hello, Doctor, I have a temperature and a headache.

4 a For 1–6, check (✓) the sentence (a or b) that is said in a more careful way. Then practice saying it.

1 a Go home, rest, and take your medicine. ☐
b I think you should go home, rest, and take your medicine. ☐

2 a Are you ready for some bad news? ☐
b I'm afraid I have some bad news. ☐

3 a Maybe it'll be best if you sit down here. ☐
b Sit down here. ☐

4 a Maybe we should call the doctor. ☐
b Call the doctor. ☐

5 a I think you should probably stay in bed. ☐
b Don't even think of getting out of bed. ☐

6 a That won't help! ☐
b Sorry, but I'm not sure that will help. ☐

b Your friend's not feeling well. Read the text and write him/her some advice.

"There's no way I can go to school tomorrow. I have a runny nose, a temperature, and a cough. I don't know what to do!"

____

5 65 PRONOUNCE Listen to the advice and underline the words that are stressed. Then practice repeating the sentences.

1 I think you should go home and rest.
2 Should I go back to bed?
3 First, you should take a pain reliever.
4 I have a stomachache and a sore throat.
5 I'm afraid I feel terrible!
6 If you take some medicine, you'll feel better.

WRITING

Give examples

1 Read the article. What is cyberbullying?

a bullying someone at school
b bullying someone on the street
c using electronic devices to bully someone

CYBERBULLYING

What do you think of when you hear the word *bully*? For a lot of kids this means someone who tries to hurt you. For example, they might hit you or push you. It also means someone who does unkind things such as calling you names. These days there's a new kind of bully who uses devices like cell phones, tablets, or computers to make other people unhappy.

There are many different kinds of cyberbullying. For example, telling lies about someone on a social network, posting photos of someone without their permission, or making cruel comments about someone on a forum. Sadly, cyberbullying is becoming more common.

If you have a problem with cyberbullying, there are a lot of things you can do. For example, first you should talk to a friend, parent, or teacher. There are also books, websites, and forums on cyberbullying where you can find advice. If the cyberbullying is very serious, you should contact the police.

2 Circle the words or phrases in the article that are used to give examples (*like*, *such as*, *for example*).

3 Find examples of the following in the article.

1 Two ways someone might hurt you:
hit you or push you
2 One way someone might be unkind to you:
......
3 Three electronic devices:
......
4 Three kinds of cyberbullying:
......
5 Three things you can do if you have a problem with cyberbullying:
......

4 Rewrite the sentences to include the examples in parentheses. Use *like*, *such as*, or *for example*.

1 I'm worried about a lot of things. (exams, argue with my best friend)
I'm worried about a lot of things, such as exams and arguing with my best friend.
2 If you have a cold, there are many things you can do to help. (drink water, rest)
......
3 You should eat healthy food. (salad, fruit, vegetables)
......
4 There are a lot of things I want for my birthday. (a phone, a soccer ball)
......
5 My dad cooks some great meals. (Spanish omelette, lemon chicken)
......
6 You can easily injure parts of your body when you play soccer. (knee, ankle)
......

5 You're going to give advice to a friend by email.

One of your friends is receiving terrible emails from a person in his/her class. Think about the problem and the advice you will give.

WRITING PLAN

Make a plan for your email.

1 Describe your friend's problem. (*I'm sorry that …*) ☐

2 Write about the results of different actions. (*If you don't … , you will … ; If you … , maybe …*) ☐

3 Give two pieces of advice. (*It's a good idea … ; You might want to … ; Maybe you should/shouldn't ..*) ☐

4 Include some examples. (*For example, like, such as*) ☐

WRITE AND CHECK

6 Write your email. Check (✓) the stages in the plan.

Communicate your message when you give a speech

1 ▶66 Listen to Mark and his sister, Maria, having a conversation at home. Mark is practicing a speech. What does he do well and what does he do badly? Put a check (✓) or an X (✗) beside each point (1–5).

1 Make eye contact with the audience. ☐
2 Don't read the speech. Use notes, or cards with a few words on them. ☐
3 Introduce the speech. Say what you're going to talk about. ☐
4 Speak slowly and clearly. ☐
5 Practice your speech. Give it to friends or family members. ☐

2 ▶67 This is Mark's finished speech. Put the sections (1–5) in the right order. Then listen and check.

___ A year ago, Toby was a happy, popular student without any real worries or problems. He was at the top of his class in every subject and really good at sports too. I guess we all wanted to be like him – maybe some of us were even a little jealous of him!

_1_ Everyone knows Toby and I are the best of friends, so I am really happy to be the person who gets to present him the award for Special Achievement at this year's Student Awards Ceremony. But before I give Toby his award, I want to say a few words about him and his special achievement.

___ But then everything changed. Toby found out he had a heart problem. He was really tired. He no longer played the sports he was so good at. But he still had courage. He organized a walk to raise money for heart research.

___ Toby, you are amazing. The walk raised $5,000, and you walked with us. You deserve this award more than anyone. Please, everyone, let's hear the applause for Toby Johnson, the winner of this year's award for Special Achievement.

___ Toby, before and after the surgery, you were still strong inside. You never gave up. When I visited you in the hospital, I was really worried about you, but you were confident. You said, "Everything will be OK. I have the best friends and family in the world. I'll be back on the field soon."

3 Think of someone you know who deserves a Special Achievement award. Make some notes about them and write a speech in your notebook. Practice it with your family or friends. Then give your speech in class.

1 Find four parts of the body and four items of clothing in the word snake. Then match the clothes to the parts of the body.

chestfeetjeanslegsheadshirthatshoes

	clothes	**parts of the body**
1	....	....
2	....	....
3	....	....
4	....	....

2 Read the clues and write the personality adjectives to complete the puzzle and find the mystery word.

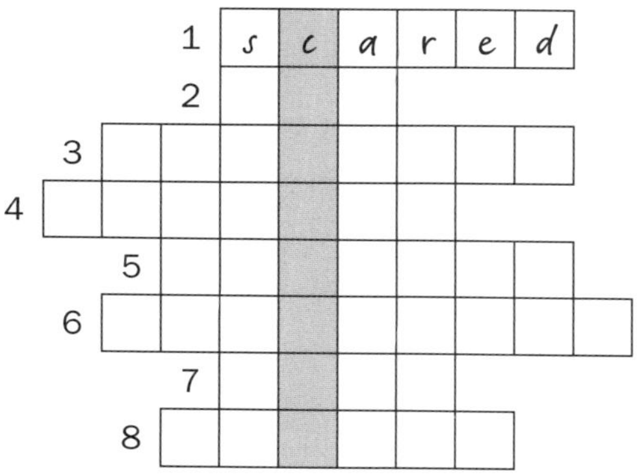

Clues

1 I'm not brave! I'm always *scared* when I'm at home alone!
2 My sister isn't .... She talks to everyone!
3 Jade's a very .... person. She always says "hello" and stops to chat.
4 I don't mind waiting at the bank or post office. I'm very ....
5 My dad's very .... He doesn't laugh very much.
6 She's good at everything, and she knows it. She's very ....
7 Emma can be a little .... ! She forgets to say "please" and "thank you."
8 My cousins are very .... They always say "please" and "thank you" when we come to visit.

Mystery word: ....

3 Choose the correct option to complete the sentences.

1 The largest ___ in the world is the Taiga. Its trees stretch from Canada to Alaska.
   a forest
   b lake
   c river
2 The Sahara is the second largest ___ in the world.
   a dessert
   b desert
   c field
3 Human beings have 10 ___ .
   a feet
   b toes
   c thumbs
4 Most ___ are nocturnal. That means they hunt at night.
   a dolphins
   b owls
   c ants
5 A giant ___ covers Antarctica.
   a field
   b savannah
   c ice sheet
6 You can't make an omelette without ___ .
   a eggs
   b soup
   c steak

4 Complete the sentences.

1 We're from Brazil so we speak P........ .
2 A small river is called a s........ .
3 She lives on the coast. Her house is near the b........ .
4 I don't eat meat – I'm a v........ .
5 They keep animals and grow vegetables on their f........ .
6 P........ are black and white birds that can't fly.
7 Our house only has one floor – it's a b........ .
8 A small, low mountain is called a h........ .

ALL ABOUT ME

1 Choose three adjectives to describe yourself.

....

2 What clothes are you wearing today?

....

3 What are your three favorite animals?

....

1 Complete the sentences with the correct form of the verbs in the box.

go meet play read send study take train

1 I like .... tennis.
2 I'm good at .... pictures.
3 He's going to .... a comic book.
4 I prefer to .... text messages.
5 He's .... his friends this afternoon.
6 He hopes he'll .... to college.
7 I'm tired of .... I have a headache.
8 They're going to .... hard to get on the team.

2 Choose the correct options to complete the blog entry.

BLOG SEARCH

I (1) ***was standing*** / ***am standing*** outside the classroom yesterday. I (2) ***waited*** / ***was waiting*** for my French teacher. It was about noon, and everyone (3) ***was having*** / ***had*** lunch. A girl from the sixth grade (4) ***came*** / ***was coming*** up to me. She (5) ***said*** / ***was saying*** some really mean things to me. She (6) ***didn't do*** / ***wasn't doing*** anything, but I was scared. I thought she might hit me. Luckily my teacher (7) ***arrived*** / ***was arriving***, and the girl (8) ***was going*** / ***went*** away.

3 Write the words in parentheses in the correct form to complete the conditional sentences.

1 If you .... (exercise) a lot, you become stronger.
2 If it rains tomorrow, we .... (definitely / not / go) to the beach.
3 If he .... (not / pass) his exams, he might not get into college next year.
4 If he uses the computer a lot, he always .... (get) a headache.
5 If you .... (switch off) completely, it helps you to relax.
6 If she goes to bed early, she .... (probably / not / be) tired the next day.

4 Complete the sentences with the correct words in the box.

a few anybody anything much nobody something

1 Did you hear .... about the accident?
2 There isn't .... time at night to watch TV.
3 I always try to eat .... before I go to school.
4 I got to school early and there was .... in class except me.
5 I usually meet .... friends on Saturdays and go to the movies.
6 He didn't see .... he knew at the party.

5 Choose the correct options to complete the conversation.

Leah: What's up Sally?
Sally: Oh, I'm really nervous. I (1) ***'m giving*** / ***give*** a speech this morning. I don't like (2) ***speaking*** / ***speak*** in front of a lot of people.
Leah: Well, don't worry. I'm sure you (3) ***'re being*** / ***'ll be*** fine. You're good at speaking.
Sally: I don't know. Do you think I (4) ***should to*** / ***should*** use notes?
Leah: Yes, but you should (5) ***looking*** / ***look*** at your audience too.
Sally: OK, thanks. I'm (6) ***practicing*** / ***going to practice*** one more time.
Leah: Well, good luck. See you later.

UNIT 7

TIME FOR WORK

VOCABULARY 1 »»» Jobs and workplaces

1 Match the jobs to the tools and equipment.

artist cleaner doctor engineer hairdresser journalist ~~mechanic~~ pilot teacher

1
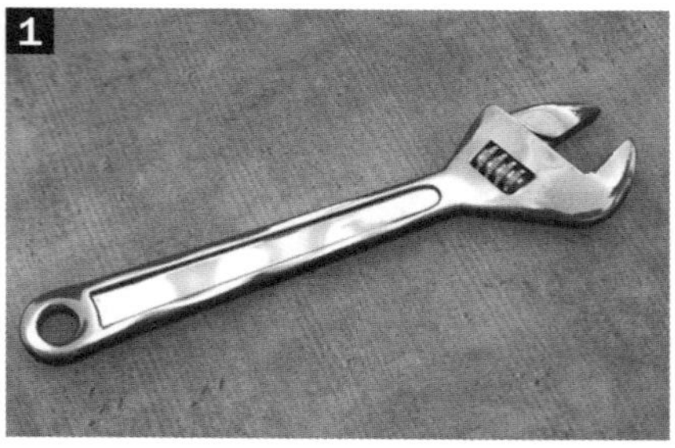
mechanic

2

....

3

....

4

....

5

....

6

....

7

....

8
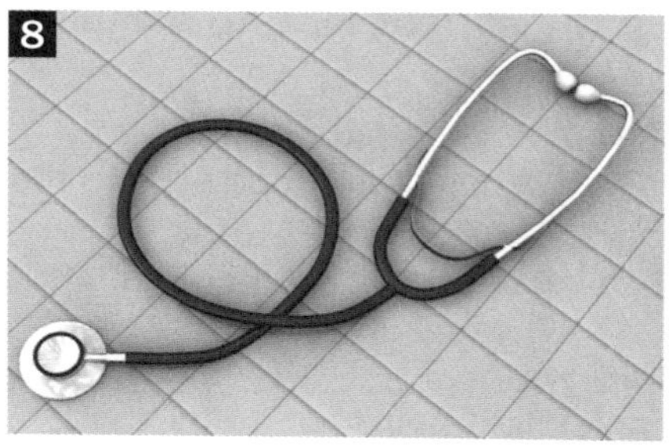
....

9

....

2 Add *-r* or *-er* to the verbs to make jobs.

1 clean cleaner
2 drive ....
3 train ....
4 farm ....
5 wait ....

3 Complete the sentences with words from Exercises 1 and 2.

1 A .... works on a farm.
2 A .... works in a hair salon.
3 A .... flies airplanes.
4 A .... works in a school.
5 A .... works in a hospital.
6 A .... works in a restaurant.

4 Write the correct jobs for each person.

1 Our cousin works in an office. She answers the phone and writes letters.
s..........
2 My sister works in a gym. She helps people to exercise and stay healthy.
f.......... t..........
3 Their brother works in a hospital. He gives medicine to the patients and helps the doctors.
n..........
4 My dad's best friend often works outside. He helps to build bridges and roads.
e..........
5 His aunt works in an office. She helps people book hotels and flights and plan their vacations.
t.......... a..........
6 Mom works in a restaurant. She makes delicious food.
c..........
7 He works in a hotel. He sits at the front desk and meets people when they arrive.
r..........
8 She works at home. She writes articles and stories, and she sells them to news websites.
j..........

READING

Identify the topic

1 Look at the pictures below. Can you guess their jobs?

Zara: **a** vet (animal doctor) **b** engineer **c** dentist
Pascale: **a** teacher **b** fitness trainer **c** ice cream maker

2 Complete the tips with the words in the box.

REMEMBER HOW TO ...

identify the topic

first quickly text topic words

- The topic of a (1) ____________ is usually in the (2) ____________ sentence. Read these (3) "____________ sentences" carefully.
- Identify important (4) ____________ in the topic sentences.
- Read the rest of each paragraph (5) ____________ .

3 Read the texts and decide which go with each person. Write *a* (Zara) or *b* (Pascale) in the first box.

4 Number the paragraphs for each text (a and b) like this:

1 A description of the job.
2 The skills that they need for the job.
3 The negative side of the job.
4 Why they like the job.

5 Read the texts again. Choose the correct option to complete the sentences.

1 Pascale thinks his job is ____ .
a varied **b** boring **c** difficult
2 He goes to the ____ three times a year.
a gym **b** university **c** dentist
3 He thinks his job is ____ .
a dangerous **b** interesting **c** difficult
4 Zara's job is to ____ animals.
a train **b** take care of **c** feed
5 Animal owners bring their animals to ____ .
a the farm **b** the zoo **c** the hospital
6 Her job can be ____ .
a boring **b** exciting **c** dangerous

6 Which job do you prefer? Why?

____

____

MOVE BEYOND

Use the internet to find out more about your dream job. Write the name of the job and three facts about it.

____

____

____

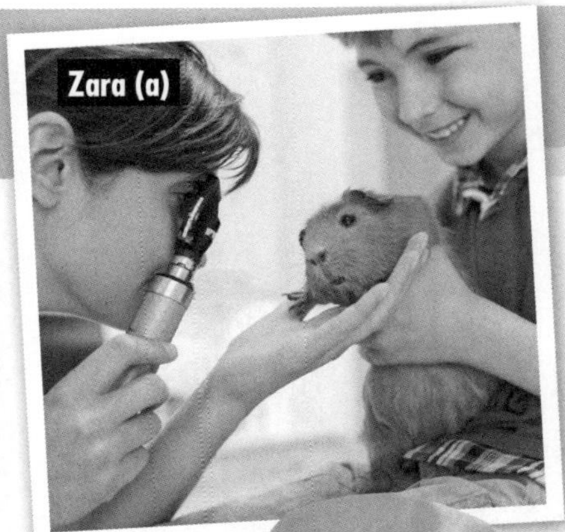

Zara (a)

Pascale (b)

DREAM JOBS

[b] [2] To get this job, I studied food science in college. After that I had to get some work experience. I worked on a dairy farm to see how they produce cream and butter. There are two important things – you must have a good sense of taste, and you must love ice cream.

[ ] [ ] The best thing about this job is when I see animals get better. I'm happy when the pet owners are happy and their animals are well again.

[ ] [ ] It's a fantastic job because I eat new kinds of ice cream every day. I have to be very creative. I also get to travel a lot, and I love that. For example, last year I went to Paris to find out about new recipes. I learned so much!

[ ] [ ] I'm a little like a cook and a little like a scientist – I don't work in a restaurant. I have to think of new flavors and ask people to taste them. That's not difficult because most people are happy to try the product!

[ ] [ ] I help take care of sick animals – like a doctor but for animals. Sometimes, I have to visit animals on farms or in the zoo. Most of the time, people bring their pets here to the animal hospital.

[ ] [ ] It's not always easy to find out what's wrong with an animal, because it can't tell you! You have to be patient. Sometimes animals bite, especially when they're scared or hurt. Sometimes they cry, which is terrible!

[ ] [ ] When I do this job, I eat a lot of sugar and fat. I have to be careful not to gain weight, so I go to the gym three times a week. I also go to the dentist every four months to make sure my teeth are OK.

[ ] [ ] First, I got a college degree in biology. After that, I had to get a degree in veterinary medicine. I had to study all kinds of animals, including birds and fish. Then I had to work for three years before I became a licensed vet.

GRAMMAR 1 *Must* and *mustn't*, *have to* and *don't have to*

Talk about things you need or don't need to do

1 Complete the grammar table with the correct forms.

must/mustn't		
Subject	***must/mustn't***	**Verb**
You	must	(1) .... sneakers to do sports.
I	(2)	be late for school.
have to/don't have to		
Subject	***have to/don't have to***	**Verb**
I	have to	call my best friend.
He	has to	(3) .... over 16 to see this movie.
You	(4) .... have to	go to school on public holidays.
She	(5) .... have to	shout – I heard her!
Past forms		
We	(6) .... to	take our pet to the vet.
They	(7) .... have to	go to school when they were sick.

2 Choose the correct option to complete the rules.

1 Use *must/have to* when something is ***necessary*** / ***forbidden***.
2 Use *mustn't* when something is ***dangerous or not allowed*** / ***not necessary***.
3 Use *don't have to* when something isn't ***allowed*** / ***necessary***.

3 Complete the texts with the words in the box.

don't have to (x3) have to must mustn't

Julio: I'm a taxi driver in New York City. I sometimes (1) .... work at night, but I (2) .... use my own car – they give me one with the job. To be a good taxi driver, you (3) .... drive carefully, and you (4) .... drive too fast. I (5) .... wear special clothes; my usual stuff is fine. I (6) .... speak other languages, but sometimes it's useful if my customers are tourists.

had to (x3) didn't have to (x2)

Susie: Last year I had a summer job as a bike messenger. I (7) .... get up early every day to deliver packages around the city. I (8) .... use my own bike – they gave me one with the job. I (9) .... wear a helmet. I (10) .... take a test for this job, but I (11) .... get a special license.

4 Use the prompts to write questions about the people in Exercise 3. Use the correct form of *have to*. Then write the answers.

Taxi driver (use present forms)

1 he / work at night
Q: ....?
A: ....

2 he / wear a uniform
Q: ....?
A: ....

3 he / drive carefully
Q: ....?
A: ....

4 What languages / speak / he
Q: ....?
A: ....

Bike messenger (use past forms)

5 When / she / get up
Q: ....?
A: ....

6 What / she / wear
Q: ....?
A: ....

7 she / take a test
Q: ....?
A: ....

8 she / get a special license
Q: ....?
A: ....

5 › **Choose the correct options to complete the school rules.**

SCHOOL RULES

1 You *must* / *mustn't* use your cell phone in class.
2 You *must* / *don't have to* listen to the teacher.
3 You *must* / *mustn't* do your homework.
4 You *have to* / *mustn't* be kind to other students.
5 You *don't have to* / *mustn't* wear a school uniform.
6 You *have to* / *mustn't* eat or drink during class.

6 ›› **Find and correct the mistakes.**

1 I has to start my new job tomorrow.
....
2 They have to work last weekend.
....
3 She not have to wear a helmet.
....
4 He don't have to speak English.
....
5 He didn't must be late for school.
....
6 We had to take an exam tomorrow.
....
7 I mustn't work when I was at school.
....
8 We must to book our vacation soon.
....

7 ›› **Complete the conversation with the words in the box.**

did didn't do (x2) don't had have must mustn't

Sam: Tell me about your new job at the computer store. What (1) .... you have to do?
Becky: A lot of different things. It's really interesting.
Sam: (2) .... you have to take a test for the job?
Becky: No, I (3) .... , but I (4) .... to answer a lot of questions about computers.
Sam: And what's the job like?
Becky: Well, it's pretty easy. I (5) .... to explain how to use the computers.
Sam: (6) .... you have to fix computer problems?
Becky: No, I (7) .... have to do that.
Sam: Could I get a job there?
Becky: Yes, I think so. I'll ask the manager tomorrow. Remember, in the interview, you (8) .... answer all the questions clearly, and you (9) .... be shy!
Sam: OK, I'll give it a try!

8 ››› **Rewrite the sentences and questions using the correct form of *have to*.**

1 I don't wear a uniform.
....
2 I speak English.
....
3 We took a test.
....
4 We didn't study music.
....
5 We worked on a ship.
....
6 Did you work in dangerous places?
....
7 What did you do?
....
8 What time did you start?
....

LISTENING

Recognize the speaker's message

1 Complete the tips with the words in the box.

REMEMBER HOW TO …

recognize a speaker's message

advice emphasizes imperatives shouldn't

1 Listen for phrases like *My* (1) ________ */ tip is …*
2 Listen for (2) ________ , *can/can't* and *should/* (3) ________ .
3 Listen for the words the speaker (4) ________ .

2 68 Listen to Andy's interview. What is his main message?

a Don't be afraid. b Don't listen to adults. c Don't waste time.

3 68 Check (✓) the expressions Andy uses. Then listen again and check.

- ☐ My advice is …
- ☐ My tip is …
- ☐ You should …
- ☐ You shouldn't …
- ☐ You must …
- ☐ You mustn't …

4 68 Listen again and complete the notes with information from the interview.

Andy's website
BizzyTeens gives advice to (1) ________ about how to start up a (2) ________ .

BizzyTeens
Andy started his first business when he was (3) ________ years old.
His website has had over (4) ________ visitors.
Teenagers can post (5) ________ and comments on the website.

Work and study
He wants to go to (6) ________ .
After that Andy wants to (7) ________ around the world and (8) ________ other teens who use his website.

5 Imagine your best friend is starting a business. Give him/her three tips.

____

____

Work and study

1 Match the words (1–8) to their meanings (a–h).

1	college	a	a job that you do every day
2	career	b	a job that you do for a few hours a week
3	semester	c	a part of the school year
4	exam	d	a serious kind of test
5	company	e	a place where young adults learn
6	part-time	f	this shows what you have studied/learned
7	degree	g	a group that employs people
8	full-time	h	a job that you do for many years

2 Complete the text with the words in the box.

career college company degree
exams full-time part-time semester

My goal is to study hard and get good grades on my (1) __________ this (2) __________ . Then I plan to go to (3) __________ and get a (4) __________ in web design. Right now I have a (5) __________ job helping my dad in his (6) __________ , but in the summer I'm going to get a (7) __________ job. The work experience will help me with my (8) __________ later.

3 Choose the correct option to complete the sentences.

1 Some students have ***part-time*** / ***full-time*** jobs on the weekend.
2 You can get information about jobs at the ***Degree*** / ***Careers*** Advising Center.
3 You can learn about computers by taking an IT ***class*** / ***company***.
4 You have to do well on your ***exams*** / ***business*** to get good grades and get into college.
5 Work experience helps you to learn about ***business*** / ***degrees***.

4 Complete the sentences. Then use the words to complete the crossword.

1 I work on Saturdays. It's a (1) __________ job.
2 I want to study medicine. It's a really interesting (2) __________ .
3 My mom goes to work every day. She has a (3) __________ job.
4 Our new school (4) __________ will start in August.
5 My uncle owns a small (5) __________ . He sells cars.
6 I need a (6) __________ , so I want to go to college.

WORDS & BEYOND

Complete the text with the words in the box.

achieve designs develop
equipment successful supports

I exercise every day – I love it! My dream is to start my own business as a fitness trainer. To (1) __________ my goal, I'll need to (2) __________ a really good business plan and buy my own sports (3) __________ . My dad is going to help me. My sister (4) __________ websites, so she'll help too. My family (5) __________ me a lot, which is fantastic. I think I will be really (6) __________ !

GRAMMAR 2 Present perfect

»» Talk about actions and events at a nonspecific time in the past

1 › Complete the grammar tables with the correct forms.

Present perfect – affirmative			
Subject	***have/has***	**Past participle**	
I, You, We, They	(1) ______	created	a new app.
She, He	(2) ______		
Present perfect – negative			
Subject	***haven't/hasn't***	**Past participle**	
I, You, We, They	(3) ______	used	an app before.
She, He	(4) ______		

Present perfect – *yes/no* questions				Short answers
Have/Has	**Subject**	**Past participle**		
(5) ______	you, we, they, I	designed	a new game?	Yes, I (6) ______ . / No, I haven't.
(7) ______	she, he			Yes, he has. / No, he (8) ______ .
Present perfect – *wh-* questions				
Question word	***have/has***	**Subject**	**Past participle**	
What	(9) ______	I, you, we, they	done?	
	(10) ______	she, he		

2 › Complete the rules. Use the tables in Exercise 1 to help you.

1 Use the present perfect for actions in the past ___ .
  a at a nonspecific time b at a specific time
2 Form the present perfect with ___ + past participle.
  a *is/are* b *has/have*
3 Make negative statements with ___ .
  a *not has/have* b *have/has not*
4 Make questions with ___
  a *Have you/Has she ...?* b *Do you/Does he ...?*

3 › Complete the table with the correct form of the verbs.

verb	past participle form
1 be	*been*
2 speak	______
3 tell	______
4 ______	given
5 write	______
6 ______	made
7 teach	______
8 ______	won

4 »› Complete the story using the present perfect form of the verbs in parentheses.

Olivia Varga from Recife, Brazil, is only 15, but she (1) *'s done* (do) more than most other teenagers her age. Olivia (2) ______ (start) an online business to help hungry people in her city. More than 3,000 people (3) ______ (visit) her website, and she (4) ______ (raise) over a million dollars for her charity. So how (5) ______ (she / do) it? "My family and friends (6) ______ (support) me a lot, and they (7) ______ (give) up a lot of their free time. It (8) ______ (not be) easy, but we (9) ______ (make) an amazing difference!"

5 »› Find and correct the mistakes.

1 Julia has design a new app.
______
2 We has bought a new computer game.
______
3 They has went to a conference.
______
4 She not have written an article before.
______
5 You have not give me your number.
______
6 They not have done this job before.
______

6 »»› Write a present perfect question for each answer.

1 Q: What ______ (do)?
  A: I've designed a new video game.
2 Q: Who ______ (help) you?
  A: My parents have supported me a lot.
3 Q: How many people ______ (buy) it?
  A: Nearly 500 people.
4 Q: What ______ (say) about it?
  A: They've told me that it's useful and fun.
5 Q: ______ (design) anything else?
  A: Yes, I have – an app to go with my game.

7 »»› What have you done in the past year? Think of three interesting things.

______
______
______

Make and react to apologies

1 a Complete the quiz answers with the sentences in the box. Then answer the quiz questions.

I forgot. I missed the bus!
I'm saving paper. um … my fish ate your book.

What's your excuse?

1 You've arranged to meet your friend in a coffee shop. You're 20 minutes late. What's your excuse?

Sorry I'm late, but …

a my watch is broken.

b ....

c uh … I lost track of time.

2 You've borrowed a book from your friend. Now your friend wants it back but you can't find it. What's your excuse?

I'm sorry, but …

a ....

b I left it on the bus.

c I'll find it some time.

3 You promised to call your friend yesterday, but you didn't call. What's your excuse?

I'm sorry, but …

a I lost your number.

b my battery died.

c ....

4 You haven't sent your friend a birthday card. What's your excuse?

I'm sorry, but …

a I sent it to another address.

b ....

c I thought it was next month.

Mostly a: It's hard to believe your excuses!

Mostly b: You are very good at making excuses. They sound real.

Mostly c: Your friends must be very patient with you!

b What is important when making excuses? Write three tips.

....

....

....

2 69 Listen and match each conversation (A, B, or C) to the correct excuse (1–3). Is the apology accepted?

1 I'm really sorry, but I've lost it.
Conversation ___
accepted / refused

2 I'm sorry, I completely forgot.
Conversation ___
accepted / refused

3 I tried to call, but there was no answer.
Conversation ___
accepted / refused

3 Match the parts of the sentences to make expressions for accepting apologies.

1	Don't	a	OK.
2	No	b	problem.
3	That's	c	doesn't matter.
4	Never	d	worry about it.
5	It	e	mind.

4 a 70 Listen to three conversations and put the sentences into the correct order.

___ I won't do it again, I promise.
___ I'm really sorry about your cell phone!
1a I'm sorry I was late for class this morning.
___ Really? I was waiting for you …
___ Sorry I didn't call you yesterday. I completely forgot.
___ That's all right. What happened? Did you oversleep?
___ Well … I left it on the bus.
___ What do you mean? Did you lose it?
___ Yes, I did.

b Imagine that you have broken a friend's computer. What's your excuse? What does your friend say?

....

....

5 71 PRONOUNCE Listen to the words. Choose the beginning sound for each word and then write the word. Then practice repeating the sounds.

1 *sk / (st) / sp* word: *start*
2 *fr / dr / tr* word: ....
3 *tr / br / pl* word: ....
4 *st / sp / sk* word: ....
5 *kr / kw / kl* word: ....

WRITING

Start and finish informal emails and letters

1 Write the phrases for starting and finishing informal email and letters in the correct column.

~~It's great to hear from you.~~ Thanks for your email. Hi, Lucy! How are you?
I want to hear all your news. Please send me a picture. See you soon!
Sorry I haven't written for a while. Sorry, I have to go now. Write soon!

Start	Finish
It's great to hear from you.	

2 Number the parts of the email in the correct order.

...... Jamie
1 Hi Lucas,
...... How are you?
...... I've been busy with my new Saturday job.
...... I help to feed the fish, birds, and other animals.
...... I have a job as an assistant in a pet shop!
...... That's not all. It was my birthday last week, and guess what?
...... I'm sending you a picture of me riding my bike.
...... I have to help my mom in the kitchen in a minute.
...... Sorry I haven't written for a while.
...... Sorry, I have to go now.
...... My parents gave me a new bike for my present!
...... Write soon! I want to read all your news.

3 Write the email from Exercise 2. Write the greeting and signature on separate lines. Check your spelling and add symbols, such as ☺ and ☹.

4 **You're going to write a short, informal email to a friend. Use the *Writing plan* to help you prepare.**

WRITING PLAN

Make notes for your answer.

1 Start your email.
Name (Who are you writing to?) ....
Start (use a "start" phrase) ....

2 Write about your new job, sport, or hobby.
What is it? ....
How often do you do it? ....
What do you have to do? ....

3 Finish your email. ....

....

Say goodbye (use a "finish" phrase). ....
Add some symbols ☺ ☹. ....

....

WRITE AND CHECK

5 **Write your email. Check (✓) the stages in the plan.**

»» Understand how different cultures think about time

1 **Read the email. Who is Marie staying with?** a h__ __t f_m__l__

Sent: Friday March 25th, 11:22 p.m.

Hi Stella,

I'm writing to you from my host house ☺. It's nearly 11:30 p.m., and we've just finished dinner! I want to go to bed, but I'm so full. Everyone goes to bed late here, but they also get up early. It was so difficult to get up this morning!

We have breakfast very early, so I'm starving by lunchtime. Luckily we have a big lunch, which is wonderful. The food is similar to what we eat at home. It's great – everyone is really relaxed and talks a lot. It is really loud at the table ☺.

Today I wanted to go shopping after lunch, but the stores are closed in the afternoon. We stayed at the house and everyone took a nap. (I definitely needed it!)

We got up around 5:00 p.m. and had some coffee. I don't usually drink coffee at that time, but I was still pretty tired. Tonight we went out shopping. We went by bus – it took a long time for the bus to arrive, but no one got angry at all!

We looked around the stores for a couple of hours – they all stay open so late here! By then I was tired and hungry, and I didn't feel like shopping. Then we came back to the house for dinner at 10:00 p.m.

It's so different from home, but I'm having a great time and the family is really friendly.

Write soon!
Marie xxxx

2 **Read the email again and answer the questions.**

1 What is different about the host country and Marie's home country?

....

2 What is the same about the host country and Marie's home country?

....

3 What things could the host family do to make Marie feel more comfortable?

....

1 Write the words in the correct circles.

ankle bear business cabinet career closet coffee crocodile degree engineer frog hall hand lemon nose onion pilot refrigerator rice sandwich sink snake stomach tooth turtle

home and furniture

work

food and drink

wildlife

parts of the body

2 Find the incorrect word in each sentence. Then rewrite it correctly. Change one word only.

1 I have a sore throat and a runny thumb. ....
2 A doctor works in a restaurant and helps sick people. ....
3 A dentist can fix your motorcycle or car. ....
4 Penguins fly at night and eat small animals. ....
5 We went swimming in the desert. ....
6 You fry potatoes in a bowl, using a little oil. ....
7 Bend down and touch the floor with your toes. ....
8 I'm not worried about my test because I'm very shy. ....

3 Complete the paragraph with words from this unit.

My name's Kristin. I live in Vancouver. My mom's very healthy, because she's a (1) f............ .... I have a (2) p............-............ job at a hair salon on Saturdays. When I finish high school, I want to go to (3) c............ to study Art because I want to be an (4) a............ or a designer. Maybe I'll have a (5) c............ in advertising, or I might try to start my own (6) c............ .

ALL ABOUT ME

1 What's your dream job? Why?

....

2 What job do you think is exciting? Why?

....

3 What job do you think is difficult? Why?

....

1 Complete the sentences with the correct (affirmative or negative) form of the verbs in the box. More than one answer may be possible.

could have to may might must should will

1 When I finish high school, I ______ study engineering, but I'm not sure.
2 There's a test tomorrow, so you ______ stay up late tonight.
3 I was sick last week and I ______ go to school.
4 To be a taxi driver, you ______ take a special driving test.
5 You're so good at sports, you ______ have a career as an athlete.
6 I probably ______ study physics because I'm not good at math.

2 Complete the conversation with the correct options.

Diane: It's 4:20 and (1) ___ here for twenty minutes!
Nick: I know … I know … I'm late again. Sorry!
Diane: What's your excuse this time?
Nick: Well, you know my dad's away on a business trip right now, so I (2) ___ finish some chores at home first. And then I (3) ___ the bus!
Diane: Oh, I see. Well, never mind. It was only (4) ___ minutes … but if you're late, you (5) ___ text me or something, OK?
Nick: Sure! But you're right, I (6) ___ late. You know in some countries, if you (7) ___ too early, they think it's not very polite.
Diane: Oh really?
Nick: Well, everyone understands that if you say one o'clock, it really (8) ___ ten past one.
Diane: Oh, I see – so everyone's always late?
Nick: Yeah, kind of … anyway, let's go – if we (9) ___ hurry, we'll miss the movie.
Diane: OK, it's a good thing I (10) ___ the tickets already!

1 a I've been b I'm c I was
2 a have to b had to c must
3 a missed b miss c have missed
4 a not much b a little c a few
5 a should b are c will
6 a am usually b usually c will be usually
7 a will be b are c should be
8 a will mean b means c mean
9 a don't b won't c shouldn't
10 a 've bought b was buying c am buying

3 Choose the correct options to complete the text.

GETTING A PART-TIME JOB

Almost (1) *anyone* / *everyone* wants to get a part-time job while they are a teenager! But how do you get a job if you don't have (2) *a few* / *any* experience? Here are (3) *a little* / *a few* simple ideas to help you get your first part-time job.

First, make a list of (4) *something* / *everything* that you're good at. Include your hobbies, sports, and free-time activities. Give (5) *some* / *a lot* examples of ways you have helped (6) *somebody* / *everybody* or created (7) *everything* / *something*. Don't forget to list tests, exams, or (8) *any* / *some* other successes. Don't leave (9) *everything* / *anything* out!

Next, make a list of places where you want to work. Do you know (10) *anyone* / *everyone* who works there? What are (11) *a little* / *some* questions you can ask them about the business?

Finally, write letters to each company, telling them about yourself. Ask a parent or a friend to check them for you. You'll soon find (12) *some* / *any* excellent job opportunities.

UNIT 8

MEDIA MIX

VOCABULARY 1 >>> Types of movies and TV shows

1 a Complete the puzzle and find the mystery word.

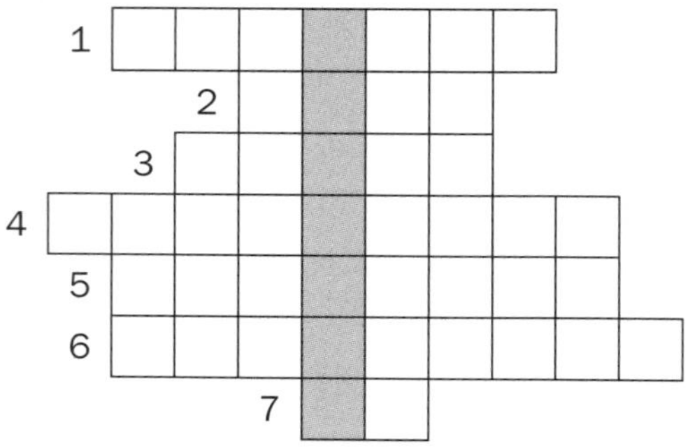

1 Something you read to find information online.
2 A thing with pages and a cover; you read it.
3 A short movie that you watch online or record on a cell phone.
4 Something you read, which uses pictures to tell stories.
5 Something you read that has a lot of photos and articles inside.
6 Something you read every day to find out what's happening.
7 A thing that you TV shows and movies on.

Mystery word: ....

b Which things in the puzzle do you use every day? ....

2 Complete the sentences with the correct form of *watch*, *read*, or *listen to*.

1 My little brother loves .... DVDs – cartoons are his favorites.
2 What kind of music are you .... ? Is that a new CD?
3 Do you ever .... the newspaper? I prefer watching TV.
4 Last night my dad .... a science fiction movie about aliens.
5 I .... a magazine called *New Horizons* – it's really interesting!
6 We often .... the news on the radio in the car.

3 Match the definitions to the correct words below.

1 People try to win prizes on this show. *f*
2 You can learn facts and new information from this show. ....
3 You can find out if it will be hot or cold tomorrow on this show. ....
4 This type of movie is made in the USA, and it's about cowboys. ....
5 Watch interviews with interesting people on this show. ....
6 Find out what's happening around the world from this show. ....

a the news
b western
c talk show
d weather
e documentary
f game show

4 a Choose the correct options to complete the conversation.

Sam: Hey Dana. What are you doing later?
Dana: I might go to the (1) ***cooking show*** / ***horror movie*** festival in the park. Do you want to come with me?
Sam: No thanks, I don't like being scared! I prefer (2) ***musicals*** / ***cartoons***, because I love singing.
Dana: OK. How about watching a (3) ***DVD*** / ***CD*** at my house then?
Sam: What do you have?
Dana: Um ... I have a (4) ***documentary*** / ***comedy*** about a journey to the bottom of the ocean and (5) ***an action*** / ***a science fiction*** movie about people living on the moon.
Sam: Hm, I'm not sure! Do you have anything funny?
Dana: Not really. I don't like (6) ***comedies*** / ***dramas***. Should we play tennis instead?
Sam: Yes, I think so!

b What kinds of movies do you like best? Why?

....

....

Identify the author's argument

1 Complete the tips with the correct words.

REMEMBER HOW TO ...

identify the author's argument

beginning   opinion   phrases   reasons   summary

- Look for the author's (1) __________ near the (2) __________ of the text.
- Then find (3) __________: look for words/ (4) __________ like *first*, *second*, or *for example*.
- Look for a (5) __________ at the end of the text.

2 Read the text below quickly. What kind of movie is *Changing Skies*?

a science fiction
b comedy
c documentary

3 Read the text again. Which part ...

1 states Sanjay's opinion? ____
2 states and supports his opinion? ____
3 gives some additional examples of why he liked the movie? ____
4 is a summary? ____

4 Number the paragraphs (A, B, C, and D) in the correct order.

5 Decide if the sentences are correct (*C*) or incorrect (*I*).

1 Sanjay is a professional movie critic. ____
2 *Changing Skies* takes place in California. ____
3 Sanjay thinks both the photography and the music are really good. ____
4 The movie is about families. ____
5 The movie was very expensive to make. ____
6 There are some famous stars in the movie. ____
7 The director has made other movies. ____
8 *Changing Skies* is a blockbuster. ____

MOVE BEYOND

Find reviews of your favorite movie online. Do you agree/disagree with the reviews? Which points do you agree/disagree with?

____
____
____
____

MOVIE CRITICS CLUB

Home • News • Reviews

Welcome to *Movie Critics Club*! On this webpage, we share our opinions on the latest movies. This week: Sanjay, a teenager living in California, writes about *Changing Skies.*

A ☐ This movie is great for a lot of reasons. First, the director's really young, and it's his first movie. He made it with only a little money. Second, it appeals to all kinds of people, because the characters are all different ages. It tells a beautiful story about families.

B ☐ In my opinion, *Changing Skies* is the best movie out this year! It's really, really good. It's a documentary about how the lives of Egyptian people have changed over the years.

C ☐ In summary, *Changing Skies* is the movie of the year because of the characters and the story and the beautiful landscape of Egypt. Go and see it right now!

D ☐ Here are some extra reasons why I liked the movie. The photography is excellent. For example, the scenes in Cairo and around the Red Sea are amazing. The music's not bad, but it's not my favorite part. The actors are also fantastic! They're ordinary people, not stars, but they do an amazing job.

GRAMMAR 1 Present perfect with *ever* and *never*

Talk about experiences

1 Complete the grammar table with the correct forms.

Present perfect sentences with *never*				
Subject	*have*	*never*	Past participle	
I/You/We/They	have ('ve)	never	eaten	with chopsticks.
He/She	(1) .... ('s)	(2)	visited	Paris.
Present perfect questions with *ever*				
Have	Subject	*ever*	Past participle	
Have	they	(3)	(4)	*Star Wars*?
(5)	she	ever	eaten	Indian food?
Short answers				
Yes, I (6) .... / No, they haven't.				
Yes, she has. / No, she (7)				

2 Choose the correct option to complete the rules. Use the table in Exercise 1 to help you.

1 Use the present perfect with ***ever*** / ***never*** to ask about experiences.
2 Use ***ever*** / ***never*** to say that you have not done something before.
3 Put ***ever*** / ***never*** before the past participle in questions.
4 Put ***ever*** / ***never*** before the past participle in affirmative sentences.

3 Write the past participles of the verbs.

1 eat ....
2 go ....
3 give ....
4 make ....
5 see ....
6 sing ....
7 do ....
8 have ....
9 be ....
10 read ....

4 a Choose the correct option to complete the sentences.

1 He ***'s*** / ***'ve*** never been to Alaska.
2 ***Have*** / ***Has*** they ever won a race?
3 Andrea and Zahara ***has*** / ***have*** never been to the beach in winter.
4 ***Have*** / ***Has*** you ever taken part in a game show?
5 ***Has*** / ***Have*** he ever studied French?
6 We ***'ve*** / ***'s*** never been ice skating.

b Think of three things you've never done.

....
....
....

5 Rearrange the words to make sentences.

1 Have / ever / you / sushi / eaten ?
....
2 has / been / She / abroad / never .
....
3 ever / he / Has / *Harry Potter* / read ?
....
4 they / classical music / to / Have / ever / listened ?
....
5 seen / she / science fiction / Has / ever / a / movie ?
....
6 never / He / late / been / has .
....

6 › **Complete the sentences with the past participles of the verbs in the box. Then complete the answers.**

have eat ~~have~~ play watch sing

1 Have you ever *had* a party? No, *I haven't* .
2 Have you ever ________ karaoke? Yes, ________ .
3 Have they ever ________ basketball? No, ________ .
4 Have you ever ________ a science fiction movie? Yes, ________ .
5 Has she ever ________ a part-time job? No, ________ .
6 Has he ever ________ a Spanish omelette? No, ________ .

7 › **Find and correct the mistakes in these sentences.**

1 Have you never seen *Star Wars*?
Have you ever seen "Star Wars"?
2 My teacher have never written anything on our class blog.
____
3 Have Mark ever listened to jazz music?
____
4 I've never play a musical instrument.
____
5 Has your father ever been to Iceland? No, he haven't.
____
6 That movie director has ever won an award.
____

8 »› **Complete the questions in the "Life experiences" Questionnaire.**

Have you ever ...

	PHILLIP	SUSANNA
1 go / Paris ? *Have you ever been to Paris?*	(✗)	(✓)
2 eat / paella ? ________	(✗)	(✓)
3 iron / a shirt ? ________	(✓)	(✗)
4 sing / karaoke ? ________	(✗)	(✓)
5 write / a web article ? ________	(✓)	(✗)
6 teach / a class ? ________	(✓)	(✗)

9 »› **What have Phillip and Susanna never done? Write sentences using the present perfect and *never*.**

1 *Phillip's never been to Paris.*
2 ________
3 ________
4 ________
5 ________
6 ________

10 »»› **Write sentences using the present perfect and *ever* or *never*.**

1 I / watch / the TV show *Ugly Betty* .
I've never watched the TV show "Ugly Betty."
2 She write / a magazine article .
____
3 John / sing / karaoke ?
____
4 they / make / Japanese sushi ?
____
5 Javier and Yasmin / eat / with chopsticks .
____
6 The company / give / money to charity .
____

Use the audio type to help you understand

1 Complete the tips with the words in the box.

REMEMBER HOW TO ...

use the audio type to help you understand

conversation information words and phrases

- Identify the audio type. Is it a (1) .... ? A speech? A news show?
- Think about the type of (2) .... you might hear.
- Listen for (3) .... you expect to hear.

2 Look at the picture and answer the questions.

1 Where is the conversation happening?
 a at school b at a café c at a hospital

2 The conversation is about podcasts. Check (✓) the words you might hear.

podcast	☐	newspaper	☐
blockbuster	☐	listen to	☐
symptom	☐	download	☐
printer	☐	stretch	☐
website	☐	watch	☐

3 ▶72 Listen and find the two types of podcasts that each person mentions. Match each person to two types of podcasts from the box.

history jokes movie reviews news stories Spanish sports news

Emma
Podcast type 1: ....
Podcast type 2: ....

Dave
Podcast type 1: ....
Podcast type 2: ....

Ryan
Podcast type 1: ....
Podcast type 2: ....

4 ▶72 Listen again and decide if these statements are correct (*C*) or incorrect (*I*).

1 Emma has downloaded podcasts onto her MP3 player. ......
2 Emma listens to podcasts every week. ......
3 Dave listens to sports news podcasts. ......
4 Dave enjoys listening to the radio. ......
5 Ryan has downloaded podcasts from an adventure website. ......
6 Their teacher enjoys podcasts too. ......

5 Do you listen to podcasts? Why or why not?

....

....

VOCABULARY 2

Crime

1 Solve the code and complete the newspaper headlines. Then match them to the pictures.

A ....

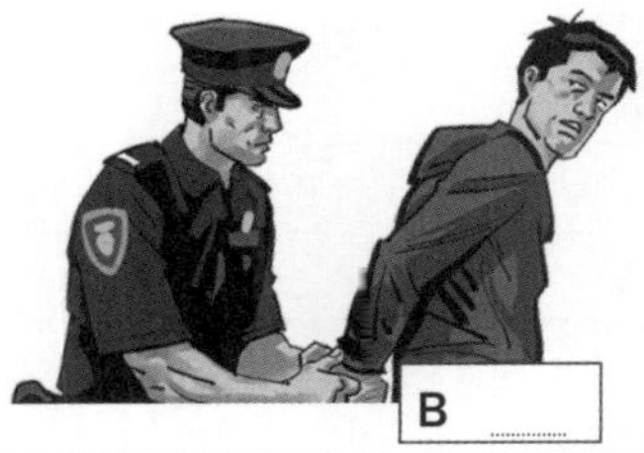

B ....

C ....

A	B	C	D	E	F	G	H	I	J	K	L	M	N	O	P	Q	R	S	T	U	V	W	X	Y	Z
26	25	24	23	22	21	20	19	18	17	16	15	14	13	12	11	10	9	8	7	6	5	4	3	2	1

1

26	14	25	6	15	26	13	24	22		26	24	24	18	23	22	13	7	

2

24	9	18	14	18	13	26	15		26	9	9	22	8	7	22	23

3

12	21	21	18	24	22	9		8	7	12	11	8		7	19	18	22	21

2 Choose the correct option to complete the sentences.

1 I saw a car ...... on Main Street yesterday.
 a traffic b accident
2 It was the top ...... on the news today.
 a story b entertainment
3 How awful! Were there any ...... ?
 a victims b thieves
4 Somebody called ...... , but luckily no one was hurt.
 a a police car b an ambulance
5 The police officers ...... two people.
 a arrested b stole
6 They took the ...... away in their police car.
 a crimes b criminals

3 Complete the news stories with the words in the box.

accident ambulance crime criminal police officer police officers thief victim

Highway accident

(1) .... arrived to help at the scene of a bad (2) .... on the highway this morning. Two vehicles crashed when one entered the highway. An (3) .... arrived a few minutes later.

THIEF STEALS HANDBAG FROM 80-YEAR-OLD

A (4) .... stole a handbag from an elderly woman on May 15. The (5) .... , who is 80, was walking in the park. She was upset but not hurt. A (6) .... later caught the (7) .... and arrested him. The officer described it as a terrible (8) ....

WORDS & BEYOND

Choose the correct option to complete the sentences.

1 Some of the ***merchandise*** / ***audience*** from the movie includes action figures and board games.
2 I didn't like the ***results*** / ***ending*** of the movie because two of the main characters died!
3 Tomorrow is the last ***episode*** / ***delay*** of my favorite TV series!
4 Everyone loved the movie. I'm sure it will be a ***series*** / ***blockbuster***!
5 This science fiction movie takes place in a ***galaxy*** / ***symbol*** somewhere in the universe.
6 Did the movie get a good ***rating*** / ***summary***?

GRAMMAR 2 Present perfect with *already*, *yet*, and *just*

›››› Talk about things related to the present

1 › Complete the grammar table with the correct forms.

Present perfect with *already* and *just* – affirmative sentences			
Subject	***have***	***already/just***	**Past participle**
I/We/They	have	just	(1) ________ (finish) the exam.
He/She	(2) ________	already	(3) ________ (see) that movie.
Present perfect with *already* and *just* – questions			
Have	**Subject**	***already/just***	**Past participle**
(4) ________	you/we/they	just	(5) ________ (be) shopping?
Has	he/she/the bus	already	(6) ________ (leave) the station?
Present perfect with *yet* – negative sentences			
Subject	***haven't/hasn't***	**Past participle**	***yet***
He/She	hasn't	called the police	yet
Present perfect with *yet* – questions			
(7) ________	(8) ________	(9) ________	(10) ________
Have	you/we/they	been to Bogota	yet?

2 › Choose the correct option to complete the rules.

a Use the ***simple past*** / ***present perfect*** with unspecific times in the past.
b Use the ***simple past*** / ***present perfect*** with specific times in the past.
c Use the ***simple past*** / ***present perfect*** with *ever/never* to talk about life experiences.
d Use the ***simple past*** / ***present perfect*** with *just*, *yet*, and *already* to talk about recent events.

3 ›› Complete the text with *already*, *yet*, and *just*.

Welcome to *News by the Minute* on WJSR.
We've (1) ________ heard that there's been an accident on the highway. It happened an hour ago. Police officers have only (2) ________ arrived at the scene. The road is not open to traffic (3) ________ , but they hope to clear it soon. Luckily, nobody was injured, and the ambulances have (4) ________ left. The police are worried. There have (5) ________ been six accidents on this highway this month. They haven't found the reason (6) ________ .

4 ›› Write present perfect sentences using the prompts and the word in parentheses.

1 the police officers / not arrest / the criminals . (yet)
____
2 you / call / the police ? (already)
____
3 someone / steal / my bag . (just)
____
4 they / catch / the criminal ? (yet)
____
5 we / call / an ambulance . (just)
____
6 I / speak / the victim . (already)
____

5 ››› Write the verbs in parentheses in the present perfect or the simple past to complete the sentences.

1 He ________ (be) a police officer for 10 years and he loves his job.
2 She ________ (be) in a car accident last year.
3 Yesterday a thief ________ (steal) her bag and ran away.
4 ________ (you / ever see) an accident?
5 The police officers arrived and ________ (arrest) the criminals.
6 I ________ (just hear) an ambulance arrive at the scene.

Agree or disagree with someone

1 Read the first part of the conversation in Exercise 2 quickly. What are the teenagers talking about?

a a TV show
b a webpage
c a podcast

2 73 Complete the conversation with the phrases in the box. Then listen and check.

agree did you think don't think I thought right totally disagree what about what you mean you're wrong

Eric: Hi Amy. We're talking about that talk show, *Speak Out!* Did you see it last night?
Amy: Ugh, yes, I did.
Eric: What (1) ________ of it?
Amy: (2) ________ it was terrible! I (3) ________ with that teacher on the show. I (4) ________ students today are lazy.
Eric: Well, I (5) ________ with him! A lot of students in our class never do their homework.
Josh: Oh, I think (6) ________ Eric! I know (7) ________ – there are a few students who don't care, but (8) ________ everyone else?
Amy: Josh is (9) ________ . In my opinion there are good students and bad ones, but we aren't all bad!
Josh: Exactly. He can't say we're all lazy. That's not fair!

3 Choose the correct answers.

1 What did Amy think of the show?
a She liked it.
b She didn't like it.

2 What did the teacher think about students today?
a He thought they were serious.
b He thought they were lazy.

3 Who agrees with the teacher?
a Amy
b Eric

4 Who agrees with Josh?
a Amy
b Eric

4 74 Number the conversation in the correct order. Then listen and check.

___ **A:** I totally disagree! I thought it was the best class we've had this year!
___ **B:** Yes, well … I don't!
___ **A:** What did you think of that English class?
___ **A:** I know what you mean. Most teens don't like stories about history, but I do!
___ **B:** You're wrong. I didn't like the book we read. It isn't very interesting for teenagers.
___ **B:** It was so boring. I nearly fell asleep.

5 75 PRONOUNCE Listen and write the words. Listen again and check (✓) the words that have a /ʧ/ sound. Then practice repeating the words.

1 *watch* ✓
2 ________ ☐
3 ________ ☐
4 ________ ☐
5 ________ ☐
6 ________ ☐
7 ________ ☐
8 ________ ☐

WRITING

Give opinions

1 Choose the best option to complete the tips.

REMEMBER HOW TO ...

give opinions

- Use phrases to (1) ***introduce*** / ***organize*** your opinions.
- Give (2) ***views*** / ***reasons*** for your opinions.
- It's (3) ***important*** / ***not important*** to give examples of something you liked and add details.

2 Read Jason's blog about a website he has found. Complete the text with the words in the box.

best main opinion Personally

Music World is the (1) .... music website I've ever been on! I like it because it's really international. It has songs and video clips from groups around the world. But, in my view, it has many other interesting features. (2) .... , I love the news section. This tells you where the hottest bands are performing and when you can buy their next CDs. There's a karaoke section, so you can sing along to the most popular songs with your family and friends! The (3).................... reason I like this site is the "New Music" section. You can listen to a lot of new bands and singers. In my (4) .... , this section is better than the radio because you can always find new music. Best of all, *Music World* is free! For all these reasons, every music fan should check out Music World!

3 Complete the notes about the website.

Name and type of website	(1)	(2) ....
Two things Jason likes about the website	(3)	(4) ....
What he likes best about the website	(5)	

4 Decide what each sentence from the blog does. Check (✓) the correct box.

	opinion	reason	example or detail
1 In my view, it has many other interesting features.	✓		
2 It has songs and video clips from groups around the world.			
3 The main reason I like this site is the "New Music" section.			
4 This section is better than the radio because you can always find new music.			
5 Best of all, *Music World* is free!			
6 There's a karaoke section so you can sing along.			
7 Personally, I love the news section.			

5 **You're going to write a short blog (one paragraph) about your favorite website. Think about a website you like and use a lot. Use the Writing Plan to help you prepare.**

WRITING PLAN

Make notes for your paragraph.

1 Type of website ______ ☐
Name of website ______ ☐
2 Two or three reasons why you like it
______
______ ☐
3 Example of something you like a lot / extra details about the website
______
______ ☐
4 Who might like this website
______ ☐
5 Finally, add phrases to introduce your opinions and reasons, and link the notes you made!

WRITE AND CHECK

6 **Now write your blog. Check (✓) the stages in the plan.**

Talk about problems

1 **Read this message from Liz to her friend Al. How does Liz feel?** ______

Received: 11:03 p.m., Friday May 28th

Hi Al,
I'm really sorry, but I can't come to the beach with your family tomorrow. I'm very stressed.
☹
Liz

2 **Imagine you are Liz. What could the problem be?**

______
______

3 **Now imagine you are Al. Answer the questions.**

1 How do you feel when you get the message? ______
2 What could Liz do to make her situation better? ______

4 **Write a reply to Liz. Include suggestions to help her talk about her problems.**

______
______
______
______
______

COMMUNICATE & COOPERATE

1 Write the words in the correct column of the table.

business career college exams keyboard mouse
printer screen semester speaker teacher webcam

Computer parts	Work and study

2 Choose the correct option to complete the sentences.

1 If you want to listen to music on the train, you should use your ***headphones*** / ***speakers***.
2 I'm going to the ***movies*** / ***swimming*** with some friends on Saturday.
3 This summer we're spending a month by ***an ocean*** / ***a lake*** in the Norwegian mountains.
4 When we were hiking in Canada last summer, we saw a big, black ***bee*** / ***bear***.
5 Is a ***turtle*** / ***shark*** a kind of fish? No, it's a reptile!
6 First, ***chop*** / ***beat*** the vegetables and boil the water.

3 For questions 1–8, choose the correct options.

1 This helps you to read at night.
a lamp b dishwasher c apps
2 This bird can swim, but it can't fly.
a crocodile b parrot c penguin
3 You use this part of the body to think, learn, and dream.
a bone b brain c knee
4 This is a device to help you do math.
a headphones b calculator c compass
5 This makes your computer documents into paper documents.
a printer b monitor c keyboard
6 You use this to clean the floor.
a iron b dishwasher c vacuum cleaner
7 This will help you find your way if you're lost.
a compass b snorkel c class schedule
8 If you're very sick, you need to go here.
a farm b hospital c hotel

ALL ABOUT ME

1 Name two things you read every day and two things you listen to every day.

2 What kinds of TV shows do you usually watch? What kinds do you never watch?

1 Complete the conversation with the present perfect or simple past form of the verbs in the parentheses.

A: (1) ______ (you / see) the new *Hunger Games* movie yet?
B: Yes, I (2) ______ (watch) it last weekend.
A: (3) ______ (you / like) it?
B: Yes, it (4) ______ (be) scary but very exciting. It's the best science fiction movie I (5) ______ (see).
A: I (6) ______ (read) the book, but I (7) ______ (see) the movie yet.
B: You should go and see it. It's very good.

2 Write negative sentences, putting the verbs into the correct tense.

1 I / not like / watch / talk shows .
______
2 He / never / see / a *James Bond* movie / before .
______
3 We / not listen / to the radio / very often .
______
4 She / not call / the police / yet .
______
5 I / not enjoy / that TV show / last night .
______
6 You / not have to / go to the movie theater / to see movies .
______

3 Choose the correct options from the box below to complete the book review.

BOOK REVIEWS ★★★★ (121)

My friends and I (1) ____ for a new book to read, and we (2) ____ this! It's a wonderful book. I (3) ____ it because it's (4) ____ and sometimes scary. It's an adventure story about a boy called Charli Ashanti who (5) ____ to find his parents. He (6) ____ speak the language of cats and makes friends with (7) ____ lions. I've already (8) ____ this book three times, and I (9) ____ read it again! If you like adventure stories, you (10) ____ this book!

1	a	were looking	b	was looking
2	a	found	b	were finding
3	a	was liking	b	like
4	a	excited	b	exciting
5	a	is trying	b	are trying
6	a	can	b	can to
7	a	much	b	some
8	a	read	b	reading
9	a	'm going to	b	have
10	a	'll love	b	love

4 Write questions for these answers.

1 Q: How often *do you listen to the radio?*
A: I listen to the radio every day.
2 Q: How many ______
A: There are 20 computers in my school.
3 Q: What ______
A: I'm watching *Toy Story 3* on my computer.
4 Q: Where ______
A: I went to the movies last night.
5 Q: What ______
A: The best movie I've ever seen is *The Hunger Games*.
6 Q: How long ______
A: A doctor has to study for about five years.

UNIT 9

SPORTS REPORT

VOCABULARY 1 >>> Sports equipment

1 Label the pictures.

1 h..........

2 r..........

3 i..........

4 fl..........

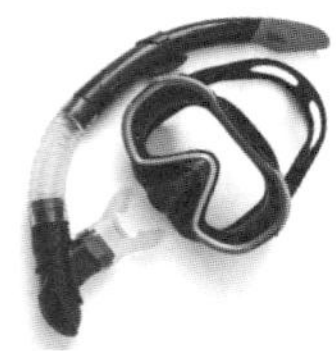
5 m..........
and sn..........

6 st..........

7 p..........

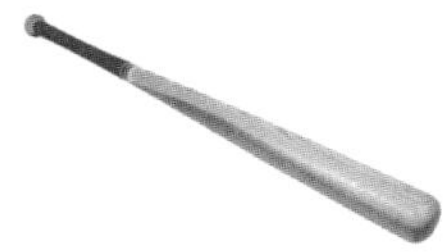
8 b..........

2 Write two pieces of equipment you need for each sport.

Basketball	Baseball	Tennis	Diving	Soccer	Volleyball
b..........	b..........	r..........	s..........	b..........	b..........
h..........	b..........	n..........	f..........	g..........	n..........

3 Write the phrases in the correct place in the circles.

two teams
two or four players
a racket
a bat or ball
a net
two goals
a helmet

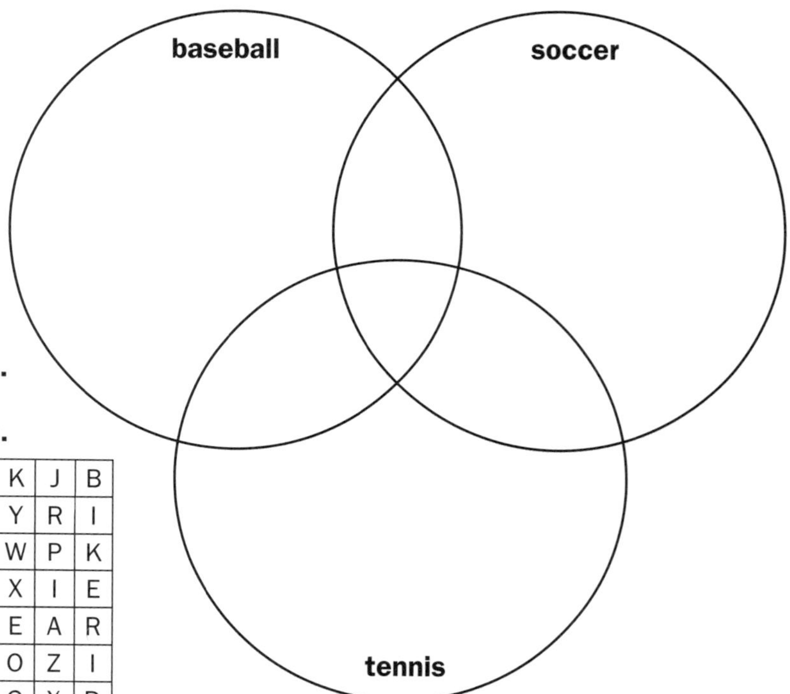

4 Write the names of the sports (1–12). Then find your answers in the word search to check that they are correct.

T	H	D	S	O	C	C	E	R	Y	Z	B	G	K	J	B
A	O	E	F	K	K	A	P	O	Y	R	N	Z	Y	R	I
B	R	N	A	T	I	C	M	Z	K	I	E	I	W	P	K
L	S	K	M	U	Y	I	R	B	T	A	K	B	X	I	E
E	E	A	S	J	H	T	N	A	V	X	R	E	E	A	R
T	B	E	R	W	F	G	K	G	T	E	Y	I	O	Z	I
E	A	O	I	L	I	S	S	U	R	F	I	N	G	X	D
N	C	Q	R	M	E	M	M	S	M	G	K	Q	E	T	I
N	K	X	W	C	Z	G	M	P	I	Y	R	N	F	M	N
I	R	B	I	R	N	O	Y	I	W	E	O	V	I	Y	G
S	I	E	A	I	E	P	T	U	N	S	Q	H	S	A	E
M	D	R	L	C	E	W	B	J	Q	G	J	U	P	I	U
I	I	C	R	E	Y	X	S	A	I	L	I	N	G	B	T
N	N	Z	V	H	M	N	G	O	L	F	I	E	Z	R	V
C	G	S	E	S	N	O	W	B	O	A	R	D	I	N	G
G	Y	M	N	A	S	T	I	C	S	J	E	P	L	S	X

Water sports
1 sa..........
2 su..........
3 sw..........

Ball sports
4 g..........
5 s..........
6 t..........
t..........

Winter sports
7 sk..........
8 sn..........
9 i.......... ....g

Other sports
10 b.......... ....g
11 gy..........
12 h..........
r..........

Understand pronouns

1 Choose the correct options to complete the tips.

REMEMBER HOW TO ...

understand pronouns

- Find the (1) ***noun* / *pronoun*** (e.g., *it/its, they/them/their*).
- Identify the correct (2) ***noun* / *pronoun*** (e.g., *sport, players*) for the pronoun. A pronoun usually comes (3) ***before* / *after*** the noun.
- Replace the pronoun with a noun. If it sounds wrong, find another (4) ***noun* / *pronoun***.

2 Read the texts and sentences 1–8 below. Which sport does each sentence match? Write *A* (Bossaball), *B* (Unicycle hockey), *AB* (Both) or *DS* (Doesn't say).

A *Bossaball* is a new sport, which first appeared in Spain in 2004. (1) **Bossaball** is popular in countries like Brazil, Germany, Singapore, Ecuador, and Saudi Arabia. The game is similar to volleyball. You can use your head, feet, or hands to hit the ball over the net. (2) **The ball** has to land in the opposite team's part of the court to win points. The first team to get 25 points wins. Bossaball takes place on a huge inflatable court with a trampoline on each side. There are 3–5 players on each team and (3) **the players** can bounce off the trampoline to hit the ball higher.

B *Unicycle hockey* is very similar to ice hockey, but all players have to ride unicycles with both feet on the pedals. (4) **Unicycle hockey** has been played since the 1920s. There are two teams of five players each. (5) **The players** use sticks and a ball and there are two goals. Players who fall off (6) **the players'** unicycles can get on again in exactly the same place. The court has no corners, and (7) **the court** has safety barriers on all sides. Unicycle hockey has fans in the UK and Germany, and (8) **unicycle hockey's** popularity is growing!

1 You can use your hands to hit the ball. ____
2 There are more than three players on a team. ____
3 It's popular in many countries. ____
4 It's a new game. ____
5 It's popular in Australia. ____
6 The rules are like volleyball. ____
7 It uses a special court. ____
8 It's difficult to learn. ____

3 Read the texts again. Write pronouns to replace the words/phrases in bold.

1 ____ 5 ____
2 ____ 6 ____
3 ____ 7 ____
4 ____ 8 ____

4 a Complete the facts about bossaball and unicycle hockey with the correct pronouns.

1 ____'s played on trampolines.
2 The players use ____ heads, feet, and hands to touch the ball.
3 ____ play until one team has scored 25 points.
4 ____ hit the ball with a stick.
5 ____'s a very fast sport.
6 The court has safety barriers all around ____.

b Which sport do you prefer? Why?

____

MOVE BEYOND

Use the internet to find out about another unusual sport. Write the name of your sport and three facts about it.

____
____
____
____

GRAMMAR 1 Relative clauses

Use relative clauses to describe people, things, and places

1 Complete the grammar table with the correct relative pronouns.

Relative clauses		
Soccer is a sport	(1) ________ / (2) ________	is popular in South America.
People	(3) ________ / (4) ________	play ice hockey have to be good at skating.
Japan is the country	(5) ________	sumo wrestling is most popular.

2 Complete the grammar rules. Use the table in Exercise 1 to help you.

1 Use relative clauses with *who* or *that* for ____ .
   a people b things c places
2 Use relative clauses with *which* or *that* for ____ .
   a people b things c places
3 Use relative clauses with *where* for ____ .
   a people b things c places

3 Read the sentences and decide if the relative clauses describe *people*, *things*, or *places*. Then choose the correct options to complete the sentences.

1 Baseball is a sport **which** / **who** is popular in North America, Mexico, and Japan. thing
2 Greece is the country **that** / **where** the first Olympics took place. ________
3 A place **where** / **which** you can go bowling is called a bowling alley. ________
4 Tennis is a sport **where** / **that** you can play indoors or outdoors. ________
5 People **which** / **who** do skydiving are not afraid of heights. ________
6 Bodyboarding and surfing are two sports **where** / **that** you can do in the ocean. ________
7 A "velodrome" is a stadium **which** / **where** you can watch bicycle racing. ________
8 The ancient Romans were possibly the first people **that** / **which** played golf. ________

4 Complete the paragraph with the correct relative pronouns.

Springfield, Massachusetts is the place (1) ________ basketball was invented. James Naismith was a Canadian sports teacher (2) ________ taught at Springfield College. He wanted a ball sport (3) ________ you could play indoors in the winter when the weather was bad. He had 18 students in his class, so he created a game (4) ________ had two teams of nine players. He wrote the first basketball rulebook in 1891. Today the game is played with two teams (5) ________ have five players each. It's an international sport and is one of the most popular sports in the world. The USA is one of the countries (6) ________ basketball is very popular. Players (7) ________ are successful can earn a lot of money.

5 › Combine the sentences below using a relative pronoun.

1 Tennis is a sport. People play in many different countries.
Tennis is a sport that people play in many different countries.

2 Tennis is a sport. It originated in the 19th century.

3 Wimbledon is a place in London. They hold a tennis competition there every year.

4 Roger Federer is a tennis player. He has won Wimbledon a lot of times.

5 The umpire is the person in charge. He decides if the ball is inside or outside the line.

6 Digital cameras are useful tools. They show the placement of the ball.

6 ›› Find and correct the mistakes.

1 Extreme sports are sports which they are usually very fast and dangerous.

2 Extreme skiing is a sport where is becoming more popular.

3 The person which first skied down Mount Everest is called Yuichiro Miura.

4 He was also the oldest person which had reached the top of Mount Everest until 2008.

5 There are many countries where extreme skiing is a popular sport there.

6 Extreme skiers are people who that doesn't get scared easily!

7 ›› Complete the sentences using a relative pronoun and the correct information from the list (a–f).

The Olympics

1 The Olympics is an international sports event ________ .

2 The Olympic flag has five rings ________ .

3 Greece is the country ________ .

4 There's a special Olympic Committee ________ .

5 Athletes ________ represent their country.

6 Athletes ________ get a gold medal.

a It decides which sports can be part of the Olympics.
b They represent the five continents.
c It takes place every four years.
d The Olympics first took place in 776 BC.
e They take part in the Olympics.
f They win first place.

8 ››› Complete the sentences using the correct pronouns and your own ideas.

1 Skateboarding is a sport ________ .

2 A referee is a person ________ .

3 The Tour de France is a bike race ________ .

4 A marathon is a running race ________ .

5 A soccer field is a place ________ .

6 Athletes are people ________ .

LISTENING

Listen for specific information

1 Complete the tips with the words in the box.

REMEMBER HOW TO ...

listen for specific information

help make notes task words

- Look at the .... Decide what you want to know.
- Think about the topic and .... you might hear. Use words in the task to .... you.
- .... as you listen if it helps you.

2 Look at the photo. What do you think this interview will be about?

3 Look at the notes and think about the missing information. Match the notes (1–5) to the information (a–e).

1 Sport: .... [*b*]
2 Event: .... [ ]
3 Who will she play in the final? .... [ ]
4 How many times has she been in the final? .... [ ]
5 How does she feel about the final? .... [ ]

a name of a person
b name of a sport
c an adjective
d a number
e name of a competition

4 ▶76 Listen and complete the missing information in Exercise 3.

5 ▶76 Listen again. Complete the sentences with the correct words in the box. You do not need all the words.

amazing depressed depressing disappointed disappointing excited relaxed relaxing worried worrying

1 Tania is not .... about the match tomorrow.
2 Her last match was ....
3 She felt .... after the last match.
4 Now she feels confident and ....
5 Her fans are .... about tomorrow's match.
6 The match will be ....

VOCABULARY 2

-ed and -ing adjectives

1 Match the situations (1–6) to the adjectives (a–f).

1 There's a soccer game on Saturday. I'm ________ .
2 I have a math test tomorrow. I'm ________ .
3 Kate's team lost the volleyball game last week. She's ________ .
4 I've played all these video games before. I'm ________ .
5 The coach is very ________ in the new tennis app.
6 Tony fell off his bike in the race. He was ________ .

a excited
b embarrassed
c depressed
d interested
e bored
f worried

2 Choose the correct option to complete the sentences.

1 We're so ***excited*** / ***exciting*** because our big game is today.
2 The final score was ***disappointed*** / ***disappointing*** because they didn't play well.
3 I never get ***bored*** / ***boring*** when I'm watching soccer.
4 It's ***embarrassed*** / ***embarrassing*** when you never win any games.
5 I'm not really ***interested*** / ***interesting*** in water sports.
6 I couldn't get tickets for the final, so I was pretty ***depressed*** / ***depressing***.

3 Complete the email with the adjectives in the box. You don't need all of the words.

amazed amazing annoyed annoying disappointed disappointing
excited exciting relaxed relaxing worried worrying

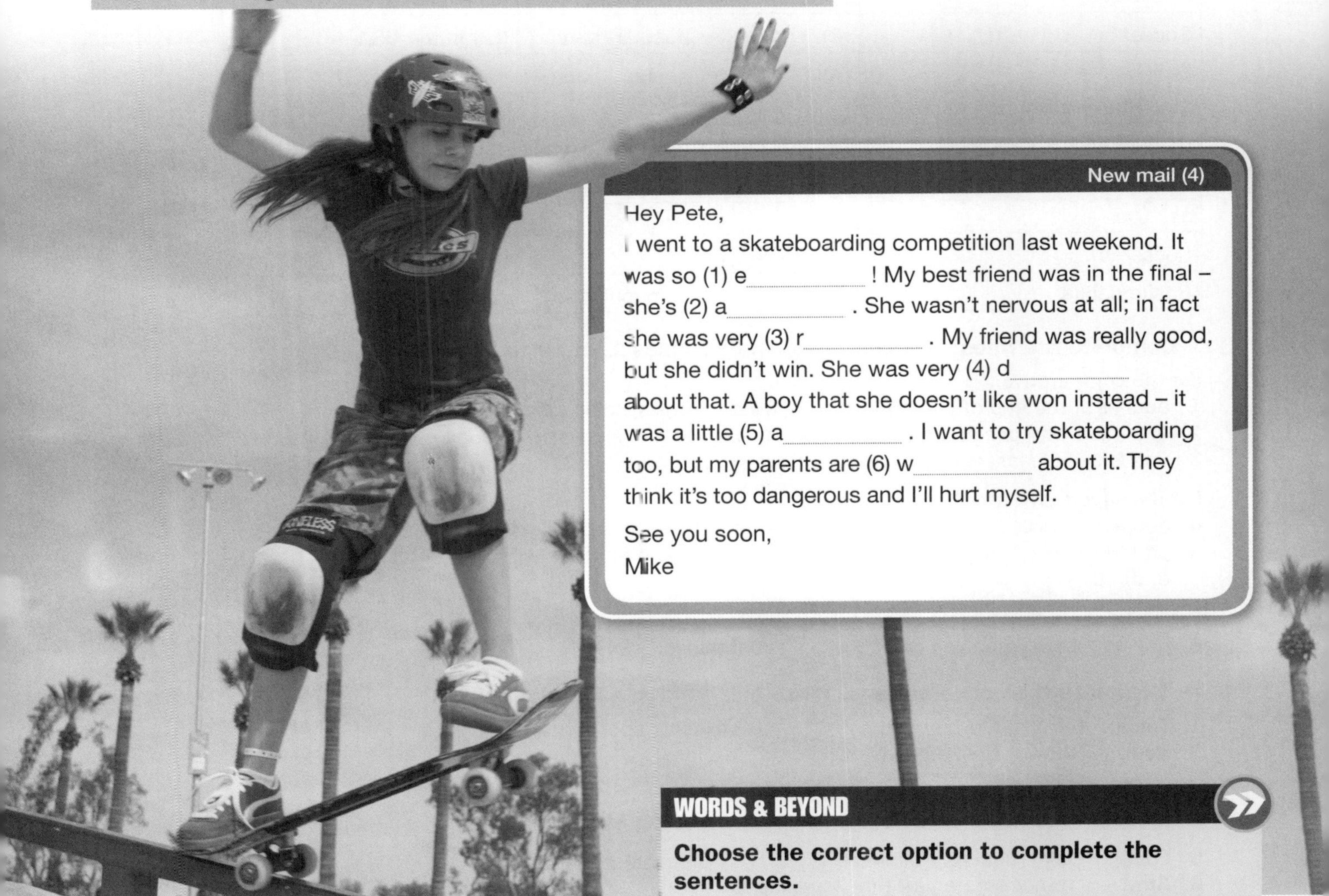

New mail (4)

Hey Pete,

I went to a skateboarding competition last weekend. It was so (1) e________ ! My best friend was in the final – she's (2) a________ . She wasn't nervous at all; in fact she was very (3) r________ . My friend was really good, but she didn't win. She was very (4) d________ about that. A boy that she doesn't like won instead – it was a little (5) a________ . I want to try skateboarding too, but my parents are (6) w________ about it. They think it's too dangerous and I'll hurt myself.

See you soon,
Mike

WORDS & BEYOND

Choose the correct option to complete the sentences.

1 The ***referee*** / ***fan*** decides who breaks the rules.
2 The team that gets the highest ***score*** / ***goal*** wins.
3 You play basketball and tennis on a ***field*** / ***court***.
4 Breathe slowly when you need to ***keep*** / ***do*** calm.
5 You play soccer and baseball on a ***field*** / ***court***.

4 How do you feel when you play or watch your favorite sport? Write three sentences.

____
____
____

GRAMMAR 2 Comparisons

Compare people, things, and places

1 › Complete the grammar table with the correct forms.

adjective	comparative form	superlative form
(1)	older	(2) ....
easy	(3)	(4) ....
(5)	(6)	the busiest
fast	(7)	(8) ....
expensive	(9)	(10) ....
(11)	more difficult	(12) ....
(13)	(14)	the best
bad	(15)	(16) ....

2 › Write the comparative and superlative form of each adjective.

Comparative adjectives		
Ice hockey is	faster (1)	baseball. (+)
Baseball is	not (2) .... fast as	ice hockey. (–)
Soccer is	(3) .... popular than	golf in the USA. (+)
Tennis is	(4) .... popular than	baseball in the USA. (–)
Superlative adjectives		
Basketball is	(5) .... most popular	sport in the USA. (+)
Hockey is	the (6) .... popular	sport in the USA. (–)
as … as		
Soccer is	as popular (7)	basketball in the USA. (=)
Basketball is	(8) .... as popular as	soccer in the UK. (–)

3 › Complete the rules. Use the tables in Exercises 1 and 2 to help you.

For the comparative …

1 add *-er* at the end of ***one-syllable adjectives / three-syllable adjectives***.
2 use *more* with ***one-syllable adjectives / two-syllable adjectives that don't end with -y***.
3 use *less* and *least* with ***one-syllable / two-syllable*** adjectives.

For the superlative …

4 add ***-est / most*** to adjectives that have one syllable or two syllables that end with *-y*.
5 add ***the + -est / the most*** to adjectives that have two or more syllables and don't end with *-y*.

For *as … as*

6 use ***as / than*** when you compare two equal things.

4 ›› Complete the conversations. Write one word in each blank.

1 **Tania**: I think volleyball is the .... exciting sport! I love it!
2 **Paul**: No way! Basketball is .... exciting!

3 **Simon**: I love tennis. I think it's the .... popular sport nowadays.
4 **Marisa**: I don't agree. It's not .... interesting as soccer.

5 **Frank**: I love running. I think it's .... healthiest sport.
6 **Amy**: I'm not sure about that. Running is .... healthy than swimming.

7 **Tina**: Do you like bike riding? I think it's the .... boring sport.
8 **Lucy**: Yes, I agree. It's the .... interesting sport for me too.

Congratulate and sympathize with people

1 Choose the option that is *not* appropriate.

1 I missed a goal and our team lost the game!
- a Never mind.
- b Better luck next time.
- (c) Good job.

2 Our volleyball team is in the final.
- a Never mind.
- b Good job!
- c Congratulations.

3 I scored thirty points in the basketball game.
- a That's amazing!
- b Fantastic!
- c Sure!

4 I hurt my leg and I couldn't play.
- a Good job.
- b That's too bad.
- c Never mind.

5 They didn't choose me for the final team.
- a Really?
- b You were amazing.
- c That's too bad.

6 I won the skateboarding competition.
- a Super!
- b Congratulations!
- c That's OK.

2 Complete the expressions with the words in the box. Then write congratulate (*C*) or sympathize (*S*).

Better	Good	I know	Never
That's	~~You did~~	You were	

1 *You did* a great job! *C*
2 ______ amazing! ___
3 ______ job! ___
4 ______ how you feel. ___
5 ______ too bad. ___
6 ______ luck next time. ___
7 ______ mind. ___

3 ▶77 Listen to the expressions from Exercise 2 and practice repeating them.

4 a ▶78 Listen to three conversations. Match the conversations (1–3) to the pictures (a–c).

a ☐

b ☐

c ☐

b Listen again and write the missing words you hear.

Conversation 1
Angie: That was an amazing game. You did a (1) ______ !
Barry: (out of breath) Thank you! It (2) ______ .
Angie: I know! The other side had a really strong team. But your team played the best. You deserved to win.

Conversation 2
Dave: Hi, what's up?
Helen: I (3) ______ the chess match again.
Dave: I know how you (4) ______ . Will you try again?
Helen: I guess so … Yes, I will.
Dave: Better (5) ______ next time.

Conversation 3
Jeff: Steve, are you OK?
Steve: Not really. I sprained my ankle, and I can't play in the game tomorrow.
Jeff: Oh, that's (6) ______ . You'll get better soon.
Steve: I hope so.

5 Complete the notes about the conversations in Exercise 4.

1 ☐ Congratulate ☐ Sympathize
Reason: *His team* ______

2 ☐ Congratulate ☐ Sympathize
Reason: *She* ______

3 ☐ Congratulate ☐ Sympathize
Reason: *He* ______

6 ▶79 PRONOUNCE Listen and underline the stress in the words. Is the stress on the first syllable (*F*) or the second (*S*)? Then practice repeating the words.

1 <u>in</u>teresting *F*
2 exciting ___
3 boring ___
4 annoying ___
5 depressing ___
6 worrying ___
7 relaxing ___
8 tiring ___

WRITING

Use pronouns

1 Write the correct pronouns to replace the bold nouns.

1 Our city's bicycle race took place last week. **The ride** took three hours and forty minutes. ____

2 A lot of people turned out to see the race. **The people** waited for several hours. ____

3 Some people came out to watch the race. Other people watched **the race** on TV. ____

4 My brother took part in the race. **My brother** came in 124th. ____

2 Read the report. Match the phrases in bold (1–5) to the language points below.

____ comparative
____ superlative
____ using commas in a list
____ relative clause to add information
1 relative clause to add information

3 Read the report again. Number the questions in the order that they are answered in the report.

____ What did you do (during the event)?
____ What kind of event was it?
____ What was the best thing?
____ Who could take part?
____ Who did you go with?
____ Why was it special or interesting?

Last weekend there was a Ciclovia bike riding event in my city. Ciclovia Day is when all the streets downtown are closed to cars. It's the safest and most relaxing day of the year. Only people (1) **who are on bicycles or on foot** can go downtown. This year I went with my (2) **mom, dad, younger sister, and aunt**. We rode our bikes downtown together. My mom and sister love bike riding. My dad and my aunt, who don't bike very often, were very tired. They stopped early for lunch!

We rode our bikes for about two hours on the main streets of our city. It was really weird because everything was so quiet! Usually the streets are crowded with cars, (3) **which make a lot of noise, dust, and pollution**. And it's too dangerous for bicycles! On Saturday the streets were very quiet and (4) **they were safer too**. People were smiling and very cheerful.

(5) **The best thing** was the picnic which we had at the end of the day with our neighbors in the city park.

4 **You are going to write a sports report. Use the *Writing plan* to help you prepare.**

WRITING PLAN

Make notes for your answer.

1 Describe the event.
Was it a game, a match, a race, or another type of sports event?

Who were the teams or players? Who did you play/go with?

Add some interesting information about them.

Where did it take place?

(Use relative clauses.)

2 Describe what happened and the result.

What was the best, worst, or most exciting moment?

3 Describe your reactions.
How did you feel during the event?

How did you feel at the end?

What will you remember about the event?

(Use comparatives and superlatives. Use pronouns.)

WRITE AND CHECK

5 **Write your report. Check (✓) the stages in the plan.**

Learn to deal with stress

KNOW YOURSELF

1 **Read the conversation. Why is Zac stressed?**

Oscar: Hey Zac, what's wrong?
Zac: It's terrible, Oscar. My dad has a new job, so we're moving to a different area. I have to change schools, and I feel so stressed about it. Every time I think about the new school, I can't breathe and I feel sick. I'm really scared of moving.
Oscar: Wow, yeah, you must be really angry too! When I feel stressed, I just play a sport. Why don't you go for a swim? You'll feel better.
Zac: I'm not sure I will. I'm really worried about this. I won't know anyone and I'll have to make new friends. I can't sleep at night because I'm worrying about the move.
Oscar: Listen, you should try and forget your problems – why don't we go to the movies this weekend? That'll help you to forget about things. Oh, and try to get eight hours of sleep at night too.
Zac: Thanks but I'm not sure how those things will help.
Oscar: Well, just tell your parents you're not moving then!

2 **Read the conversation again and answer the questions.**

1 Find the four pieces of advice that Oscar gives. ______
2 Does Oscar give good advice? Why or why not? ______

3 **What advice would you give Zac to help him deal with his problem?**

1 Choose the correct option to complete the sentences.

1 You play soccer on a ____ .
a court
b field
c lane

2 You need a ____ to play baseball.
a net
b snorkel
c bat

3 You need ____ to go snorkeling.
a skates
b flippers
c rackets

4 It's ____ to lose a game.
a amazing
b disappointing
c exciting

5 A(n) ____ flies a plane.
a mechanic
b engineer
c pilot

6 You book your vacation at a travel ____ .
a salon
b agency
c factory

7 You wear a helmet on your ____ .
a chest
b back
c head

8 People in ____ speak Spanish.
a Portugal
b France
c Mexico

9 People who always want to win are ____ .
a calm
b competitive
c generous

10 You usually buy jam in a ____ .
a box
b package
c jar

11 To make a cake, you need to ____ sugar and butter together.
a boil
b fry
c beat

12 Carrots and onions are types of ____ .
a vegetables
b fruit
c drinks

13 Crocodiles, snakes, and turtles are types of ____ .
a insects
b birds
c reptiles

14 A savannah is a place with a lot of ____ .
a ice
b trees
c grass

15 You use a ____ to keep things cold.
a refrigerator
b kettle
c cabinet

16 You use a ____ to surf the internet.
a webcam
b browser
c mouse

2 Find the odd word out. Write why it's different.

1	carrot	onion	potato	banana
2	hand	leg	helmet	arm
3	driver	stove	cleaner	writer
4	stomach	cough	cold	headache
5	racket	book	bat	hoop
6	shy	friendly	amazing	confident
7	bear	fish	turtle	lake
8	package	carton	yogurt	can
9	cleaning	vacuuming	skating	ironing
10	western	web page	comedy	cartoon

3 Match the verbs (1–8) to the nouns (a–h).

1 go	a the table
2 fly	b friends
3 throw	c horseback riding
4 cook	d a magazine
5 read	e a game
6 meet	f a ball
7 set	g a meal
8 play	h a plane

4 Complete the sentences with the correct phrases from Exercise 3. You don't need all the phrases.

1 I can ____________ from one side of a soccer field to the other.
2 I usually ____________ at the sports center on Saturday mornings and we go swimming together.
3 I love outdoor sports, and I ____________ every weekend.
4 It's my birthday, and my mom is going to ____________ for me and my friends.
5 It's my brother's job to ____________ before dinner.
6 My favorite team is going to ____________ tomorrow.

ALL ABOUT ME

1 **What sports do you love or hate? Why?**

2 **What's the most unusual sport you have tried? What was it like?**

3 **What sports do you want to try? Why?**

1 Complete the paragraph with the words in the box.

easier	smaller	the fastest	warmer	which	which is	who

Squash is a sport (1) .... played in a small court with high walls. You hit the ball against three sides of the court. The ball is made from a kind of rubber (2) .... gets (3) .... as you play. The racket is (4) .... than a tennis racket and it has a longer handle. Some people think that squash is (5) .... than tennis. It's one of (6) .... racket sports in the world. People (7) .... play at the international level can earn a lot of money from prizes and advertising contracts.

2 Choose the correct options from the box below to complete the conversation.

Suzanne: Hi Emily, are you OK? You look depressed.
Emily: Oh, I'm not depressed but I'm really tired.
Suzanne: (1) ___ enough sleep last night?
Emily: I was at basketball practice last night. We (2) ___ an important game next week, and we really want to win ... but it's so hard to keep up with my schoolwork. So I (3) ___ up really late last night because I (4) ___ my homework. Our homework is (5) ___ than last year, and I don't have enough time!
Suzanne: Have you talked to the coach about it (6) ___ ?
Emily: If I tell the coach, (7) ___ me from the team!
Suzanne: You need to talk to someone (8) ___ can help you. How about talking to your teachers?
Emily: That's not a bad idea. If I (9) ___ them about basketball practice, they might give me less homework!
Suzanne: Sure, but isn't your schoolwork (10) ___ than your basketball practice?

	a	b	c
1	Do you have	Did you get	Were you getting
2	play	're playing	played
3	stayed	was staying	've stayed
4	did	've done	was doing
5	as difficult	less difficult	more difficult
6	yet	ever	just
7	he cuts	he'll cut	he's cutting
8	which	where	who
9	'll tell	tell	told
10	more important	the most important	as important

3 Rearrange the words to make sentences.

1 The Red Sox / the Yankees / better / were / today / than .
....
2 you / ice hockey / must / when / wear / play / You / a helmet .
....
3 the / We / league / in / best / the / are / team .
....
4 never / golf / have / played / I .
....
5 play / you / If / healthy / you / be / regularly / will / sports .
....
6 interested / sport / a / new / I / in / am .
....

4 Find and correct the mistakes.

1 I'm excited in watching the bike race next week. ....
2 Tennis is a sport who has fans in England, Australia, and Spain. ....
3 Skydiving is the most excited sport I have ever done. ....
4 Robert and Sue are going to playing ice hockey next week. ....
5 We not have to wear helmets when we go running. ....
6 I want to be a professional soccer player because I practice every day. ....

10 BRAINWAVES

UNIT

VOCABULARY 1 >>> Invention verbs and materials

1 a Match the pictures to the correct words.

1 stairs ☐ 2 restrooms ☐ 3 coffee shop ☐ 4 ticket office ☐ 5 elevator ☐ 6 gift shop ☐

b Think of another place or sign you might find in a museum.

....

2 Complete the sentences with words from Exercise 1.

1 If there's a fire, you shouldn't take the *elevator* .
2 You should take the .... if there's a fire.
3 Let's meet at the .... for a drink before looking around the museum.
4 I'm going to buy some souvenirs at the ....
5 **A:** Excuse me, where are the .... ?
B: In front of the coffee shop, next to the elevators.
6 If you want to see the exhibition, arrive at the museum early.
The .... opens at 9:00 a.m.

3 a Write the words to complete the sentences in the boxes.

1 You can get maps at the .... desk.	*i*	*n*	*f*	*o*	*r*	*m*	*a*	*t*	*i*	*o*	*n*
2 The coffee shop is near the entrance on the .... floor.											
3 So many things are made of .... , like cars, bikes, soft drink cans, and paper clips.											
4 The table is made from a tree, so it's made of											
5 Water bottles, printers, and pens are usually made of											
6 Use the .... to go to the second floor.											
7 Windows are usually made of											

b Rearrange the gray letters from 3a to complete the sentence.

Telescopes are used to _ _ _ _ _ _ _ _ new planets.

4 Write one more thing made of wood, plastic, and metal.

Wood: ....
Plastic: ....
Metal: ....

5 Complete the quiz with the correct form of the verbs from the box. Then take the quiz.

build	design	discover
explore	invent	produce

How's your modern history?

Find out with our history quiz!

1 In 1980 Mount Saint Helens erupted and .... a huge cloud of smoke, ash, and gases. Where did this happen?
a in the USA b in the Philippines c in Chile
2 They built the Hubble Space Telescope to .... new information about …
a the sun. b galaxies and the universe. c Earth.
3 Zaha Hadid has .... a lot of buildings, such as the Guangzhou Opera House in China. Where is she from?
a Morocco b Yemen c Iraq
4 In 1995 the Russian cosmonaut Valeri Polyakov .... space for a record number of days. How long was he there?
a almost 438 days b almost 350 days c almost 212 days
5 Facebook® is popular right now, but who .... it?
a Alexander Graham Bell b Mark Zuckerberg c Steve Jobs
6 They .... the Golden Gate Bridge between …
a 1933 and 1937. b 1945 and 1947. c 1963 and 1967.

Use pictures for help with new words

1 Complete the tips with the words in the box.

REMEMBER HOW TO ...

use pictures for help with new words

pictures text word

- Look at the (1) .... What do they show? What's the text about?
- Read the (2) .... When you see a new (3) .... , look at the pictures. Can you see the word in the pictures?

2 Look at the title of the article and the pictures. What is the text about?

a computer monitors
b flat screen TVs
c cell phones

3 Read the text. Match the phrases (1–4) below to the pictures (a–d).

1 flat screen TV screen
2 fluorescent tube
3 neon and xenon gases
4 atoms release energy

4 Read the text again. Decide if these statements are correct (*C*) or incorrect (*I*).

1 Televisions have changed over the years. C
2 They developed the first flat screen TV in 1984. ......
3 Today flat screen TVs only produce two colors. ......
4 Flat screen TVs are made of two sheets of glass with gases between them. ......
5 Today, flat screen TVs are heavy. ......

MOVE BEYOND

Choose an object from the list below and use the internet to find out how it works. Write notes below.

radio calculator printer

....
....
....
....

HOW DO FLAT SCREEN TELEVISIONS WORK?

IN THE BEGINNING

How have televisions changed over the years? Have you ever seen a very big flat screen TV? It might seem like flat screen televisions are something new, but actually they produced the very first flat screen television back in 1964.
The difference is that the first flat screen television screens could only produce two colors. Nowadays high-definition screens are used, so this isn't a problem.

WHAT ARE THEY MADE OF?

Flat screen television screens are made from two sheets of glass. Between the glass there are neon and xenon gases. When you switch on the television, the electricity mixes with the gases, and atoms release energy. The energy creates the colored lights which make the TV picture. They work like fluorescent tubes.

WHY FLAT SCREEN TVs?

People like flat screen televisions because they aren't heavy and they don't take up much space. They are also popular because you can hang them on the wall. One possible problem is that some flat screen TV screens are very bright, which means they need more electricity.

a

b

c

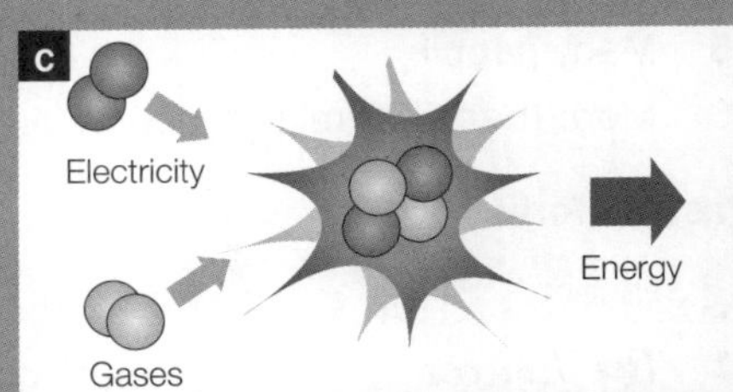

d

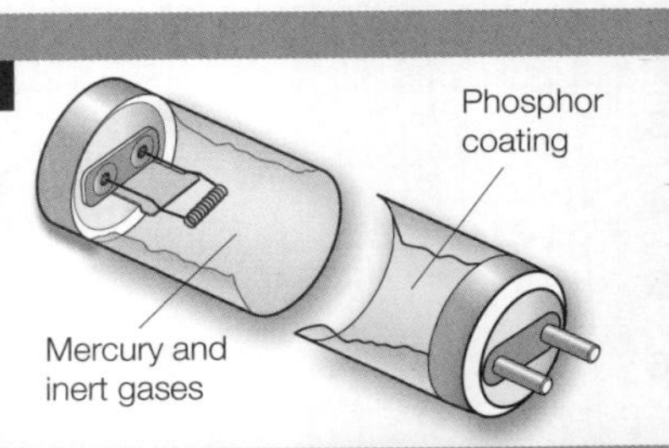

GRAMMAR 1 Simple present passive

>>> Use the simple present passive to talk about facts and processes

1 Complete the grammar table with the correct forms.

Simple present passive – affirmative sentences			
Subject	**Present of *be***	**Past participle**	
The software	(1)	created	by designers.
Chemicals	(2)	used	to make paints.
Simple present passive – negative sentences			
Subject	**Present of *be* + *not***	**Past participle**	
I	(3)	made	of stone!
Paper money	(4)	sent	over the internet.
Simple present passive – *yes/no* questions			
Present of *be*	**Subject**	**Past participle**	
(5)	glass	used	to make TV screens?
(6)	houses	built	from plastic?
Simple present passive – *wh-* questions			
Question word	**Present of *be***	**Subject**	**Past participle**
What	is	it	made from?

2 Complete the sentences with the nouns in the box.

a paper clip cell phones different parts
radio signals telescopes the museum

1 Many .... are needed to make a phone.
2 .... are used to discover new planets.
3 .... are sent by cell phones to a base station.
4 .... is usually made of plastic or metal.
5 Most .... are made in China.
6 .... is located on Main Street near the post office.

3 Rewrite the active sentences to complete the passive table.

Active form

	Subject	Verb	Object
1	Scientists	calculate	the figures.
2	Designers	create	the software.
3	Teenagers	send	many text messages.
4	Scientists	discover	new planets every day.
5	Many people	buy	tablet computers each year.
6	More than 600 million people	speak	Spanish.

Passive form

	Object	Verb	Agent (subject)
1	*The figures*	*are calculated*	*by scientists.*
2			
3			
4			.... *every day.*
5			.... *each year.*
6			

4 › Write the past participle of the verbs in the correct column.

~~find~~ make need present recycle send test throw away

Regular	Irregular
	found

5 › Choose the correct option to complete the questions.

1 What are cell phones made from?
ⓐ are / made b are / making c is / made
2 What ______ telescopes ______ for?
a are / calculated b are / used c are / using
3 How many television screens ______ ______?
a do recycle b is recycled c are recycled
4 Who ______ the designs ______ by?
a is / chosen b are / chose c are / chosen
5 What sports ______ ______ with a ball and stick?
a are playing b are played c have played
6 Where ______ the phones ______?
a do / sell b are / selling c are / sold

6 »› Complete the sentences with the correct present passive form of the verb in parentheses.

1 The windows ______ (not clean) very often.
2 Omelettes ______ (make) with eggs.
3 Computers ______ (use) in all the classrooms.
4 ______ sports ______ (play) in the afternoons at your school?
5 They ______ (make) in Korea.
6 The apps ______ (download) onto your phone.

7 »»› Write sentences using the simple present passive.

1 These elevators / design / for seniors .
______
2 Cell phones / make / of plastic and metal .
______
3 A lot of meat / eat / in Argentina ?
______
4 Cell phones / use / more than / landline phones .
______
5 The phones / not send / to the stores at first .
______
6 The history museum / not visit / very much in winter .
______

8 a »»› Read the riddle. What is the object?

It's made of plastic and metal. It contains some dangerous chemicals. It's used to send messages. It's used to make calls. What is it?
It's a ______

b Now write your own riddle using the simple present passive.

______
______
______

LISTENING

Understand new words

1 Choose the best option to complete the tips.

REMEMBER HOW TO ...

understand new words

- (1) ***Don't*** / ***First***, look at any pictures or visuals and read the task. (2) ***Predict*** / ***Listen*** words you might hear.
- Use (3) ***new*** / ***familiar*** words to help you understand the main ideas.
- (4) ***Don't stop*** / ***Stop*** listening when you hear words you don't understand.

2 Look at the photos. What do you think the listening will be about? Choose the correct option.

a glass blowing   b space technology   c making bread

a

b

c

d

3 a Match the photos (a–d) to the words and phrases below (1–4).

1 the sand is heated ☐   2 furnace ☐
3 liquid glass ☐   4 blow into the blowpipe ☐

b 80 Now listen and repeat.

4 81 Listen to the complete interview with Sylvano and decide whether the sentences are correct (*C*) or incorrect (*I*).

1 Sylvano lives on an island. ......
2 He has just started glass blowing. ......
3 He helped his father when he was younger. ......
4 The sand changes to liquid glass when it's heated. ......
5 Sylvano blows into the blowpipe. ......
6 The glass must be cool when you're creating different shapes. ......

5 81 Complete the phrases from the interview. Listen and check.

1 I think it's .... a blowpipe in English.
2 You .... the blowpipe .... change the shape of the glass.

6 Think of four objects that you use every day. Write phrases starting with:

It's used for ...
I think the ... is useful because ...

....
....
....
....

VOCABULARY 2

Everyday objects

1 Match the words to form compound nouns.

1	light	a	cap
2	bottle	b	tack
3	paper	c	pen
4	thumb	d	bulb
5	ballpoint	e	pin
6	clothes	f	clip

2 Label the pictures with the compound nouns from Exercise 1.

1 ______

2 ______

3 ______

4 ______

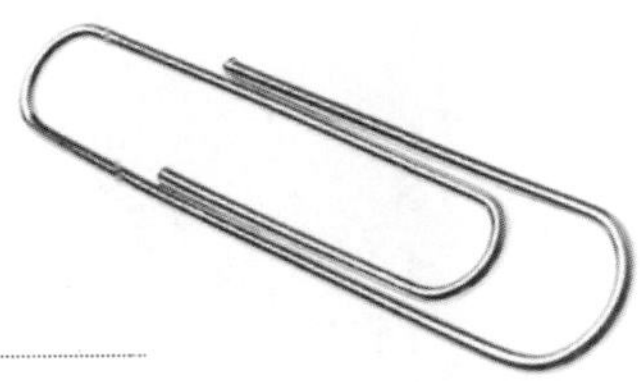

5 ______

6 *light bulb*

3 Think of two more useful everyday objects. ______ ______

4 Complete the sentences with the names of everyday objects.

1 If you're sick, you use a t_ e___ o_ e___ r to take your temperature.
2 Most people write with b_____ p____ nt pens these days. In the old days, they had to fill pens with ink.
3 Metal p_____ r c____ ps are used to hold pieces of paper together.
4 It's easier to correct your mistakes if you draw with a p______ l , not a pen.
5 S______ y n_ t___ are made of paper. You can make notes on them.
6 You put glass l_____ t b_____ s in lamps, so that you can read at night.

WORDS & BEYOND

Match the words (1–6) to the definitions (a–f).

1	ink	a	Something that sends out or receives signals.
2	network	b	Everyday object used to tie things together.
3	antenna	c	Colored liquid used for writing.
4	microchip	d	Very small part found in a computer.
5	telescope	e	Interconnected computers.
6	string	f	Something that is used to see objects at a distance.

GRAMMAR Simple past passive

»» Use the simple past passive to talk about completed actions in the past

1 › Complete the grammar table with the correct forms.

Simple past passive – affirmative sentences			
Subject	**Simple past of *be***	**Past participle**	
The can	(1) ______	invented	in 1809.
Ballpoint pens	(2) ______	invented	in 1935.
Simple past passive – negative sentences			
Subject	**Simple past of *be* + *not***	**Past participle**	
The clothespin	(3) ______	invented	in the USA.
Ballpoint pens	(4) ______	used	in the 1920s.
Simple past passive – *yes/no* questions			
Simple past of *be*	**Subject**	**Past participle**	
(5) ______	the clothespin	invented	in the USA?
(6) ______	ballpoint pens	made	in 1920?
Simple past passive – *wh-* questions			
Question word	**Simple past of *be***	**Subject**	**Past participle**
Where	was	the clothespin	invented?

2 › Choose the correct option to complete the sentences.

1 The Hubble Space Telescope ***designed* / *was designed*** to explore our galaxy.
2 Scientists ***created* / *were created*** the new computer components.
3 The Science Museum ***was built* / *built*** in 1989.
4 At first, X-rays ***weren't understood* / *didn't understand*** very well.
5 They ***didn't discover* / *wasn't discovered*** penicillin until 1928.
6 The first rockets ***made* / *were made*** in China.

3 »» Write the verbs in parentheses in the simple past passive.

1 The bridge ______ (build) by a Peruvian architect.
2 The telescopes ______ (not / design) in China.
3 The phones ______ (send) to the stores last Friday.
4 ______ the plans ______ (present) at the meeting?
5 The internet ______ (invent) in the 1980s.
6 The Modern History Museum ______ (open) in 2003.

4 a »» Complete the text with the past passive form of the verbs in the box.

create design inspire make not build open visit

The Modern History Museum

1st floor: Amazing Architects!

On the 1st floor there's an exhibition on architects from around the world. This month we have a special exhibition about the architect Zaha Hadid. The Guangzhou Opera House in China (1) ______ by Hadid, and is one of her most famous works. The building (2) ______ from concrete, metal, and glass. It (3) ______ very quickly – it took over five years. Finally, it (4) ______ in May 2010. Last year the beautiful building (5) ______ by thousands of tourists. The design for the Glasgow Riverside Museum of Transport (6) ______ also ______ by Hadid. The designs for these buildings (7) ______ by rivers and water.

b »»» Write questions about the text with the past passive.

1 Who / the Guangzhou Opera House / design / by ?

______

2 What / it / make / from ?

______

3 When / it / open ?

______

4 Who / the Glasgow Riverside Museum / design / by ?

______

5 What / the designs / inspire / by ?

______

SPEAKING

Describe things when you don't know the English word

1 ▶82 **Listen to the conversation. What does Mina need? Check (✓) the correct picture.**

a ☐

b ☐
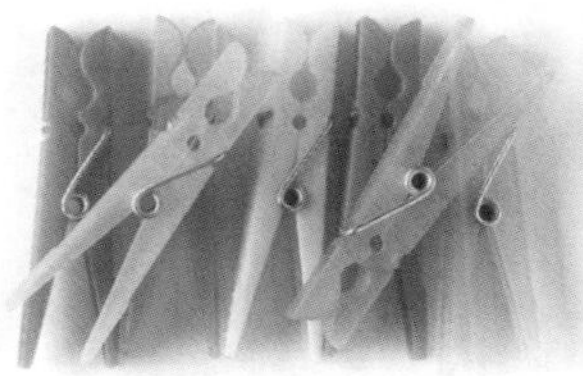

c ☐

d ☐
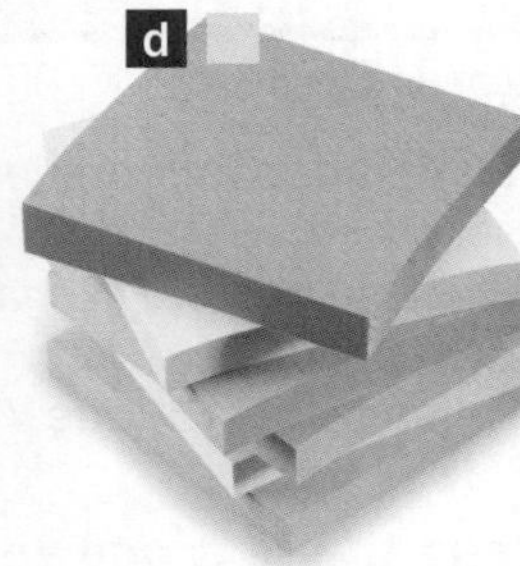

2 ▶82 **Choose the correct options to complete the conversation. Then listen again and check.**

Mina: Hi Eric! Thanks for coming shopping with me!
Eric: No problem, Mina. What do you (1) ***need*** / ***know*** to buy?
Mina: Well, I need (2) ***something*** / ***everything*** for my clothes. I don't know (3) ***what*** / ***if*** they're called.
Eric: Do you (4) ***mean*** / ***have*** a suitcase?
Mina: No, no, no! You (5) ***use*** / ***make*** them for drying clothes after you've washed them. They're small and they're (6) ***created*** / ***made*** from wood or plastic.
Eric: Oh, I know! Some clothespins, right? Like these?
Mina: Yes! Exactly! Perfect Eric. I'll take the plastic ones.
Eric: (7) ***How much*** / ***How many*** are the clothespins, please?
Clerk: They're $2.50 for a package. Is that all you need?
Mina: Yes, thank you. That's all.

3 Complete the sentences with the words in the box.

know need that wood writing

1 I ________ four, please.
2 It's small, long and it's made of ________ .
3 It's used for ________ or drawing.
4 How much is ________ , please?
5 I don't ________ what it's called.

4 Complete the conversation using the sentences in Exercise 3.

A: What do you need?
B: *I don't know what it's called.*
A: Describe it to me.
B: ________
A: What's it used for?
B: ________
A: How many do you need?
B: ________
A: Here you are.
B: ________
A: That's eight dollars, please.

5 a ▶83 PRONOUNCE **Listen to the pairs of words. Which word in each pair has the /v/ sound, *a* or *b*? Choose the correct letter.**

1 a b 3 a b 5 a b
2 a b 4 a b 6 a b

b ▶84 **Listen and practice repeating the words.**

WRITING

Present an argument

1 Choose the correct option to complete the tips.

REMEMBER HOW TO ...

present an argument

- Summarize your argument in the (1) ***first / last*** sentence.
- Give one or more (2) ***paragraphs / reasons*** to support your argument.
- Finish with a (3) ***title / conclusion***.

2 Read the text and write the phrases in the correct place.

Another reason   In conclusion
In my opinion   One reason

The most useful everyday object

(1) .... , the most useful everyday object is the ballpoint pen. You can get ballpoint pens in a lot of different colors but mainly red, blue, and black. Most people use a ballpoint pen every day of their lives.
(2) .... I've chosen the ballpoint pen is because I use them a lot. I use them to write shopping lists and memos, do homework, do crosswords, and a lot of other things. (3) .... for choosing it is that it's small and you can put it anywhere, for example in your bag or your pocket. (4) .... , there are many useful everyday objects, but the ballpoint pen is used more than most other things, and it's used for so many different things. It helps you to study, play, and to organize your life.

3 Read the text again and complete the notes in the plan with the phrases in the box.

ballpoint pen   every day   small and practical
use it a lot   use it more than other things

Object – (1) ....
How often you use it – (2) ....
Reason 1 – (3) ....
Reason 2 - (4) ....
Conclusion – (5) ....

4 Rearrange the words to make sentences.

1 useful / is / most / in my opinion / The / everyday object / ballpoint pen / the .
....
2 it / chose / I / use / One of the reasons / is / I / it / every day / because .
....
3 it / because / and / small / Another reason / like / is / practical / it / I / is .
....
4 organize your life / helps / It / to study / you / and .
....
5 it / is / In conclusion / everyday / most / useful / the / object .
....

5 **You're going to write about what you think the most useful everyday object is. Make notes for your paragraph in the *Writing plan*.**

WRITING PLAN

Make notes for your answer.

1 Say what object you have chosen and why. Use *In my opinion ...*
Object: ....
Why: ....

2 Give your first reason. Use *One of the reasons ...*
....

3 Give additional reasons. Use *Another reason ...*
....

4 Think of a conclusion. Use *In conclusion ...*
....

WRITE AND CHECK

6 **Write your paragraph. Check (✓) the stages in the plan.**

Share and exchange new ideas

1 **Amy's teacher has asked groups to brainstorm ideas for a gadget to learn English. Read Amy's feedback for her group to the rest of the class. What idea did they choose?** ....

Amy:
Jan and I both thought of some ideas really quickly. Tom had an idea, but we didn't understand it, so we didn't write that one down. Ed had an idea, but it was bad and Magda didn't say anything, but it was OK as our ideas were both good. In the end we decided to combine our ideas. We agreed on a robot that can help with pronunciation and also translate for you.

Ed:
Actually I think my idea is good, but we didn't spend enough time discussing it.

2 **Read Amy's feedback again and answer the questions.**

1 What things did they do well when they brainstormed ideas as a group?
....

2 What things could they do better next time?
....

3 **Imagine you're going to join Amy's group to brainstorm ideas for an app to learn English. Follow these steps:**

1 Write down your own ideas to contribute.
2 Look at the list of things that the group did badly in Exercise 2. Brainstorm things you can say and do to help the group do the task better this time.

....
....
....
....

1 Write the words in the correct column of the chart.

balls cheerful clear the table do the ironing friendly funny helmet hoops light bulb load the dishwasher make your bed paper clip racket serious shy skates thermometer

Sports equipment	Personality adjectives	Household chores	Everyday objects

2 Complete the sentences with words from Exercise 1.

1 If you want to be safe when riding your bike, you should wear a ______ .
2 Tennis players have six ______ in their bags when they play matches.
3 After dinner I clear the table and ______ with the dirty plates.
4 Is he confident and friendly? No, he's very ______ and serious.
5 He's very ______ . He's always in a good mood.
6 Do you have a ______ ? I need to take my temperature.

3 Look at the objects in the box. Match the objects to their owners.

1 journalist *newspaper*
2 cook ______
3 cleaner ______
4 student ______
5 doctor ______
6 driver ______

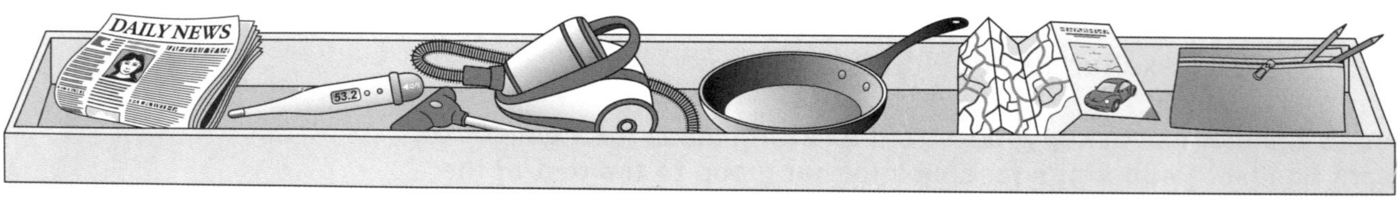

4 Choose the correct options to complete the facts.

1 The first ___ was invented in 1935 by the Hungarian brothers László and György Bíró.
a ballpoint pen b clothespin c thumbtack
2 Nicolas Appert, a chef in Paris, invented the ___ in 1809. He used it to keep food for the army.
a clothespin b can c calculator
3 The American inventor, Thomas Alva Edison, invented the ___ .
a light bulb b electricity c lamp
4 This is called a drawing pin in British English but in American English it's called a ___ .
a paper clip b thumbtack c ballpoint pen
5 In the old days, clothespins were made of ___ .
a plastic b metal c wood
6 The ___ was invented by an Italian called Marconi in 1895.
a radio b flat screen TV c laptop

ALL ABOUT ME

1 **Name three important modern inventions in your opinion.**

______

2 **Have you been to a museum recently? What did you see there?**

______

3 **Is there a museum in your town? What can you see there?**

______

1 Write the verbs in the correct tense: simple present, present progressive, present perfect, or simple present passive.

1 Webcams ________ (make) of plastic, metal, and glass.
2 He hardly ever ________ (listen to) music on his computer.
3 Right now they ________ (watch) a soap opera at Amina's house.
4 ________ you ever ________ (eat) with chopsticks?
5 The signal ________ (send) to your cell phone using an antenna.
6 **A:** ________ you ________ (study) for your history test now?
B: No, I'm watching a talk show on our new flat screen television.
7 ________ your cousin ________ (live) on a houseboat?
8 The police officers ________ (not arrest) the thief yet.

2 Choose the correct option to complete the sentences.

1 When I ***was walking*** / ***walked*** to school I saw an accident.
2 Electric cars ***invented*** / ***were invented*** many years ago.
3 ***Did you go*** / ***Were you going*** to the movies last night?
4 She ***didn't design*** / ***wasn't designed*** the Science Museum.
5 They ***watch*** / ***were watching*** TV when they suddenly heard a loud noise.
6 ***Were the designs created*** / ***Did they create the designs*** by the engineers?

3 Complete the sentences with the comparative or superlative form of the words in parentheses. Use the present tense.

1 Ballpoint pens / clothespins . (useful)
Ballpoint pens are more useful than clothespins.
2 *Toy Story* / movie I've ever seen . (good)
____
3 Computers / invention of the last 100 years . (important)
____
4 A pen / a laptop . (small)
____
5 The Science Museum / the History Museum . (interesting)
____
6 Laptops / tablets . (expensive)
____
7 The Golden Gate Bridge / bridge in the world . (beautiful)
____
8 Chess / game I've ever played . (difficult)
____

4 Complete the sentences with the verbs in the box. Use the correct future tense, *will* or *going to*.

buy	go	live	not use	see	visit

1 In the future people ________ to the moon on vacation.
2 Fifty years from now people ________ clothespins.
3 We ________ the Science Museum on the weekend.
4 After we've looked around the museum, I ________ something from the gift shop.
5 In 60 years, people ________ longer and be healthier.
6 ________ you ________ the space exhibition or the inventions?

5 Choose the correct options from the box below to complete the text.

Modern technology (1) ___ over the years. In my opinion, there are (2) ___ interesting recent innovations, but my favorite is social networking sites. One of the reasons I love them is because I can (3) ___ photos and information with my friends. Last night I (4) ___ some photos from our excursion to the Modern History Museum and I (5) ___ a post on the most interesting things we saw. Another reason I think social networking sites are important is because people can share news stories. Last month some interesting articles (6) ___ to my page and people commented on them. Finally, social networking sites (7) ___ by some people to find jobs or promote their companies. In conclusion, when I (8) ___ of an important modern day innovation, I think of social networking!

1	a	has changed	b	have changed
2	a	much	b	a lot of
3	a	to share	b	share
4	a	uploaded	b	am uploading
5	a	wrote	b	were writing
6	a	were linking	b	were linked
7	a	are used	b	use
8	a	think	b	am thinking

Macmillan Education
4 Crinan Street
London N1 9XW
A division of Macmillan Publishers Limited

Companies and representatives throughout the world

ISBN 978-1-380-00775-9

Go Beyond First published 2015
First edition entitled *Beyond* published 2014

Designed by EMC Design Ltd.

Illustrated by Peter Cornwell p. 48–49; Venitia Dean (Advocate Art) p. 59; Cyrus Deboo p. 6; Mark Duffin p. 55(tr); Sally Elford pp. 4 (banner), 14–15 (banner), 16 (banner), 26, 36–37 (banner) 38 (banner), 48 (banner/icons), 58–59 (banner), 65–69 (icons); Guy Francis (Shannon Associates) p. 57; Bob Lea pp. 4–5, 35; Chris Pavely pp. 7, 8, 13, 23, 30; Zara Picken pp. 16, 43.

Cover design by EMC Design Ltd.
Cover photograph by Getty Images/F1online/parasola parasola
Picture research by Tessa Hammond and Emily Taylor

The authors would like to thank all the team at Macmillan for everything they have done to make *Move Beyond* possible. We would like to thank Studio8 Ltd. and John Marshall Media, Inc. for their creative work on the videos, and the actors who bring the material to life. We would also like to thank John Marshall Media, Inc. for the production of the audio material. We would also like to thank all the teachers and other individuals who have contributed to the course whose names appear on this page. We would like to express a special thank you to Paige Rohrick and her parents for all their help and the interview on page 143. Finally, we would like thank our friends and families for all their support.

The authors and publishers would like to express thanks to all those who contributed to the development and formation of *Move Beyond*. In particular, we would like to thank the following teachers, contacts, and reviewers: Cristina Moisén Antón, Argelia Solis Arriaga, Krzysztof Bartold, Paweł Bienert, Agnieszka Bojanowska, Samuel Gómez Borobia, Ma. Eugenia Fernandez Castro, Jolanta Chojnacka, Elsa Georgina Cruz, Dominika Dąbrowska, Barbara Dawidowska, Galina Dragunova, Monika Drygiel-Kobylińska, Mauricio Duran, Natalia Evdokimenko, Maria Teresa Velazquez Evers, Marciana Loma-Osorio Fontecha, Monika Fromiczew-Droździńska, Patricia Garcia, Axel Morales Garcia, Miguel Angel Rodriguez Garcia, Aleksandra Gilewska, Joanna Góra, Ewa Górka, Agata Helwich, Bethsabe Ruiz Herrera, Robert Jadachowski, Patricia Guzman Luis Juan, Anna Kacpura, Ruth Kanter, Regina Kaźmierczuk, Katarzyna Konisiewicz, Maria Koprowska, Bogusława Krajewska, Aldona Krasoń, Joanna Worobiec Kugaj, Joanna Kuligowska, Tadeusz Kur, Maria Kwiatkowska, Josefina Maitret, Claire Manners, Laura Elena Medina, Carmen García Méndez, Iwona Mikucka, Talhia Miranda, Claudia Rangel Miranda, Armando Nieto, Joanna Nowak, Anna Nowakowska, Ewa Nowicka, Anastasia Parshikova, Paloma Carrasco Peñalba, Ma. Del Carmen Fernandez Perez, Joanna Płatos, Maria Teresa Portillo, Juan Jose Gomez Ramirez, Aida Rivera, Gabriela Rubio, Gabriela Bourge Ruiz, Irina Sakharova, Małgorzata Sałaj, Patricia Avila Sanchez, Jessica Galvan Sanchez, Miguel Angel Santiago, Karol Sęk, Barbara Sibilska, Tatiana Sinyavina, Agnieszka Śliwowska, Vlada Songailene, Ángela Siles Suárez, Beata Świątkowska, Ewelina Szmyd-Patuła, Agnieszka Szymaniak, José Luis Vázquez, Irma Velazquez, Małgorzata Walczak, Dariusz Winiarek, Justyna Zdunek, Zofia Żdżarska, Dominika Zięba, Marzena Zieleniewska, Anna Zielińska-Miszczuk, Robert Zielonka.

The authors and publishers would like to thank the following for permission to reproduce their images:

Farhad Acidwalla p. 21(cr);
Alamy/© ACE STOCK LIMITED p. 40(t), Alamy/Toby Adamson pp. 16–17, Alamy/Michael Flippo p. 39(7), Alamy/Glasshouse Images p. 55(a), Alamy/D. Hurst pp. 52(j), 56(microwave), Alamy/Lamb p. 52(h), Alamy/Lenscap p. 52(e), Alamy/Janet Lindsay p. 46(r), Alamy/Winston Link p. 52(d), Alamy/Magelanic Clouds p. 55(e), Alamy/Myrleen Pearson p. 23(b), Alamy/PhotoEdit p. 39(9), Alamy/Photos12 p. 29, Alamy/Radius Images p. 42(tr), Alamy/Simon Rawley p. 44(tl), Alamy/Razorpix p. 56(MP3 player), Alamy/Stargatechris p. 55(c), Alamy/Alex Stokes p. 56(tv), Alamy/Peter Stroumtsos p. 39(10), Alamy/Nicholas Stubbs p. 39(6), Alamy/Superstock p. 55(f), Alamy/Andrew Woodley p. 72;
BananaStock p. 56(boy);
Corbis/Colin Anderson/Blend Images p. 27(f), Corbis/Jamie Budge p. 27(l), Corbis/Jim Craigmyle p. 23(c), Corbis/Ian Hooton/Science Photo Library p. 22(tr), Corbis/Image Source pp. 37, 42(cr), Corbis/Christopher Little p. 27(d), Corbis/Walter Lockwood p. 40(b), Corbis/Lawrence Manning p. 39(5), Corbis/Newmann p. 19(tl), Corbis/Ocean p. 45(e), Corbis/Radius Images p. 31, Corbis/Jeff Vanuga p. 26(i);
Getty Images pp. 39(8, 12), 52(i), Getty Images/AFP/Ge p. 46(l), Getty Images/Carlos Alvarez p. 52(g), Getty Images/Blend Images – Moxie Productions p. 45(a), Getty Images/Bloomberg via Getty Images p. 27(c), Getty Images/Mark Chivers p. 58, Getty Images/ColorBlind Images LLC p. 45(d), Getty Images/Cultura/Frank and Helena p. 39, Getty Images/Cultura/Zero Creatives p. 45(b), Getty Images/Peter Dazeley p. 51, Getty Images/Jonathan Kantor p. 55(b), Getty Images/Dorling Kindersley p. 55(d), Getty Images/George Doyle p. 22(tl), Getty Images/DreamPictures p. 27(br, g), Getty Images/Flickr Open p. 52(b), Getty Images/Flickr RF p. 26(e), Getty Images/Jules Frazier p. 39(1), Getty Images/fStop p. 52(f), Getty Images/ImageSource pp. 27(b), 50(t), Getty Images/Holger Leue p. 71, Getty Images/Vincenzo Lombardo p. 56(phone), Getty Images/David Madison p. 39(4), Getty Images/Moodboard RF p. 19(cr), Getty Images/Krystian Nawrocki p. 56(microchip), Getty Images/Gary John Norman p. 27(j), Getty Images/OCA p. 39(tr), Getty Images/PhotoAlto p. 10, Getty Images/Sports Illustrated Classic p. 41(tr), Getty Images/SSPL pp. 52(a), 53(tl), Getty Images/Vetta p. 27(k);
Glow Images/Mickael David p. 18(cl), Glow Images/DreamPictures p. 18(tr), Glow Images/Stefan Obermeier p. 50(br);
Image Source pp. 27(h), 52(c), 53(tm);
Heather Lawrence/Nicely Framed p. 38;
Lucas Films Ltd./Star Wars: Episode III – Revenge of the Sith © & ™ 2005 Lucasfilm Ltd. All rights reserved. Used under authorization. Unauthorized duplication is a violation of applicable law p. 28(bl);
Macmillan Publishers Limited p. 56(web page), Macmillan Publishers Limited/Paul Bricknell p. 23(t);
Plain Picture/PhotoAlto p. 32, Plain Picture/Pictorium p. 41(br);
Press Association p. 21(tl);
Rex Features/© 20th Century Fox/Everett p. 34(tl), Rex Features/Nicholas Bailey p. 53(bl), Rex Features/© BuenaVista/Everett p. 34(b), Rex Features/© Col Pics/Everett p. 28(cm), Rex Features/© DreamWorks/Everett p. 34(tr), Rex Features/© Paramount/Everett p. 28(cr), Rex Features/© Walt Disney/Everett p. 28(tr) Rex Features/© Warner Br/Everett p. 26(a);
Paige Rohrick p. 20(tr, cl, cr);
Superstock/age footstock p. 45(c);
Thinkstock/ iStock pp. 14, 33, 39(2, 11), 44(r), Thinkstock/Monkey Business p. 44(c), Thinkstock/Hemera Technologies p. 39(3), Thinkstock/Stockbyte p. 50(cr).

Commissioned photographs by Studio8 Ltd. p. 21

Printed and bound in China

2021 2020 2019 2018 2017
10 9 8 7 6 5 4 3 2 1